BERLITZ®

RUSSIAN
FOR TRAVELLERS

By the staff of Berlitz Guides

Copyright © 1973 by Berlitz Guides, a division of Macmillan S.A.

All rights reserved. No part of this book may be reproduced or transmitted in any form or by any means, electronic or mechanical, including photocopying, recording or by any information storage and retrieval system, without permission in writing from the Publisher.

Library of Congress Catalog Card Number: 73-2271

16th printing 1989

Printed in Hungary

Berlitz Trademark Reg. U.S. Patent Office and other countries—Marca Registrada

Berlitz Guides
Avenue d'Ouchy 61
1000 Lausanne 6, Switzerland

Preface

You are about to visit the Soviet Union. Our aim is to give you a practical phrase book to help you on your trip.

Russian for Travellers provides:

* all the phrases and supplementary vocabulary you will need on your trip

* a wide variety of tourist and travel facts, tips and useful information

* a complete phonetic transcription, showing you the pronunciation of all the words and phrases listed

* special sections showing the replies your listener might give to you. Just hand him the book and let him point to the appropriate phrase. This is especially practical in certain difficult situations (doctor, car mechanic, etc.). It makes direct, quick and sure communication possible

* a logical system of presentation so that you can find the right phrase for the immediate situation

* quick reference through colour coding. The major features of the contents are on the back cover; a complete index is given inside.

These are just a few of the practical advantages. In addition, the book will prove a valuable introduction to life in the Soviet Union.

There is a comprehensive section on Eating Out, giving translations and explanations for practically anything one would find on a menu in the Soviet Union; there is a complete Shopping Guide that will enable you to obtain virtually anything you want. Trouble with the car? Turn to the mechanic's manual with its dual-language instructions. Feeling ill? Our medical section provides the most rapid communication possible between you and the doctor.

To make the most of *Russian for Travellers,* we suggest that you start with the "Guide to Pronunciation". Then go on to "Some Basic Expressions". This not only gives you a minimum vocabulary; it helps you to pronounce the language.

We are particularly grateful to Mr. Simon Markis for his help in the preparation of this book and to Dr. T. J. A. Bennett who devised the phonetic transcription. We also wish to thank Intourist, the Soviet travel bureau, for its assistance.

We shall be very pleased to receive any comments, criticisms and suggestions that you think may help us in preparing future editions.

Thank you. Have a good trip.

Throughout this book, the symbols illustrated here indicate small sections where phrases have been compiled that your foreign listener might like to say to *you*. If you don't understand him, give him the book and let him point to the phrase in his language. The English translation is just beside it.

Guide to pronunciation

The alphabet

The column at the left shows printed capital and small letters while the center column shows handwritten capital and small letters. The right-hand column will help you to pronounce the names of these letters in Russian.

А а	*А а*	ah	Р р	*Р р*	ehr
Б б	*Б б*	beh	С с	*С с*	ehs
В в	*В в*	veh	Т т	*Т т*	teh
Г г	*Г г*	geh	У у	*У у*	oo
Д д	*Д д*	deh	Ф ф	*Ф ф*	ehf
Е е	*Е е*	yeh	Х х	*Х х*	khah
Ё ё	*Ё ё*	yoh	Ц ц	*Ц ц*	tseh
Ж ж	*Ж ж*	zheh	Ч ч	*Ч ч*	chah
З з	*З з*	zeh	Ш ш	*Ш ш*	shah
И и	*И и*	ee	Щ щ	*Щ щ*	shchah
Й й	*Й й*	ee **kraht**koyeh	Ъ ъ	*ъ*	**tvyor**diy znahk (yehr)
К к	*К к*	kah			
Л л	*Л л*	ehl	Ы ы	*ы*	i (yeh**ri**)
М м	*М м*	ehm	Ь ь	*ь*	**myah**keey znahk (yehr')
Н н	*Н н*	ehn			
О о	*О о*	o	Э э	*Э э*	eh ahbah**rot**nahyeh
П п	*П п*	peh	Ю ю	*Ю ю*	yoo
			Я я	*Я я*	yah

This, of course, is not enough to pronounce Russian. We're offering you a helping hand by providing "imitated pronunciation" throughout this book. This and the following chapter are intended to make you familiar with the transcription we devised and to help you get used to the sounds of Russian.

An outline of the sounds of Russian

The imitated pronunciation should be read as if it were English, except for any special rules set out below. Letters in bold print should be read with more stress (louder) than the others.

We have chosen to give you a transcription in imitated pronunciation because the pronunciation of vowels in Russian varies considerably according to the stress. Of course, the sounds of any two languages are never exactly the same; but if you follow carefully the indications supplied here, you will have no difficulty in reading our transcriptions in such a way as to make yourself understood. After that, listening to native speakers and constant practice will help you to improve your accent.

PRONUNCIATION

Vowels

Letter	Approximate pronunciation	Symbol	Example	
а	between the **a** in c**a**t and the **ar** in c**ar**t	ah	как	kahk
е	like **ye** in **ye**t	yeh	где	gdyeh
ё	like **yo** in **yo**nder	yo	мёд	myod
и	like **ee** in s**ee**	ee	синий	**see**neey

й	like **y** in gay or boy	y	бой	boy
о	like **o** in hot	o	стол	stol
у	like **oo** in boot	oo	улица	**oo**leetsah
ы	similar to **i** in hit	i	вы	vi
э	like **e** in met	eh	эта	**eh**tah
ю	like **u** in duke	yoo	юг	yoog
я	like **ya** in yard	yah	мясо	**myah**ssah

Consonants

б	like **b** in bit	b	был	bil
в	like **v** in vine	v	ваш	vahsh
г	like **g** in go	g	город	**go**rahd
д	like **d** in do	d	да	dah
ж	like **s** in pleasure	zh	жаркий	**zhahr**keey
з	like **z** in zoo	z	за	zah
к	like **k** in kitten	k	карта	**kahr**tah
л	like **l** in lose	l	лампа	**lahm**pah
м	like **m** in my	m	масло	**mahs**lah
н	like **n** in not	n	нет	nyeht
п	like **p** in pot	p	парк	pahrk
р	like **r** in run	r	русский	**roos**keey
с	like **s** in see	s/ss	слово	**slo**vah
т	like **t** in tip	t	там	tahm
ф	like **f** in face	f	ферма	**fyehr**mah
х	like **ch** in Scottish loch	kh	хлеб	khlyehb
ц	like **ts** in sits	ts	цена	tsi**nah**
ч	like **ch** in chip	ch	час	chyahss
ш	like **sh** in shut	sh	ваша	**vah**shah
щ	like **sh** followed by **ch**	shch	щётка	**shchyot**kah

Other letters

ь   gives a "soft" pronunciation to the preceding consonant. A similar effect can be produced by pronouncing **y** as in **yet**—but very, very short—after the consonant. In our transcription we shall show this with an apostrophe (') after the soft consonant.

ъ   is sometimes used between two parts of a compound word, when the second part begins with **я**, **ю**, or **е**, to show that the pronunciation of the word should incorporate a clear separation of the two parts.

Diphthongs

The following stressed diphthongs exist in Russian:

ай	like **igh** in s**igh**	igh	май	migh
яй	like the previous sound, but preceded by the y in y**es**	yigh	негодяй	nyeegah**dyigh**
ой	like **oy** in b**oy**	oy	вой	voy
ей	like **ya** in **Ya**tes	yay	соловей	sahlah**vyay**
ый	like **i** in b**i**t followed by the y in y**es**	iy	красивый	krah**ssee**viy
уй	like **oo** in g**oo**d followed by the y in y**es**	ooy	дуй	dooy
юй	like the previous sound, but preceded by the y in y**es**	yooy	плюй	plyooy

The effects of non-stress

If a vowel or diphthong is not stressed, it often changes its pronunciation. This could be called a weakening of the sound.

| о | unstressed, is pronounced like Russian **a** | ah | отец | ah**tyehts** |
| е, я, ей, ий | unstressed, are pronounced like a short **yee** sound | yee or ee | теперь | tyee**pyehr'** |

Some basic expressions

Yes.	**Да.**	dah
No.	**Нет.**	nyeht
Please.	**Пожалуйста.**	pah**zhah**loostah
Thank you.	**Спасибо.**	spah**ssee**bah
Thank you very much.	**Большое спасибо.**	bahl'**sho**yee spah**ssee**bah
That's all right.	**Не за что.**	nyeh zah shto

Greetings

Good morning.	**Доброе утро.**	**do**brahyee **oo**trah
Good afternoon.	**Добрый день.**	**do**briy dyehn'
Good evening.	**Добрый вечер.**	**do**briy **vyeh**chyeer
Good night.	**Спокойной ночи.**	spah**koy**nigh **no**chyee
Good-bye.	**До свидания.**	dah sveeda**hnee**yah
See you later.	**До скорой встречи.**	dah **sko**righ **vstryeh**chyee
This is Mr. ...	**Это господин...**	**eh**tah gahspah**deen**
This is Mrs. ...	**Это госпожа...**	**eh**tah gahspah**zhah**
This is Miss ...	**Это госпожа...**	**eh**tah gahspah**zhah**
I'm very pleased to meet you.	**Очень приятно познакомиться.**	**o**chyeen' pree**yaht**nah pahznah**ko**mitsah
How are you?	**Как дела?**	kahk dyeh**lah**
Very well, thank you.	**Спасибо, хорошо.**	spah**ssee**bah khahrah**sho**
And you?	**А у Вас?**	ah oo vahss
Fine.	**Прекрасно.**	pryee**krahs**nah
Excuse me.	**Простите.**	prah**stee**tyee

Questions

Where?	**Где?**	gdyeh
Where is ...?	**Где...?**	gdyeh
Where are ...?	**Где...?**	gdyeh
When?	**Когда?**	kahg**dah**
What?	**Что?**	shto
How?	**Как?**	kahk
How much?	**Сколько?**	**skol**'kah
How many?	**Сколько?**	**skol**'kah
Who?	**Кто?**	kto
Why?	**Почему?**	pahch'yee**moo**
Which?	**Какой?**	kah**koy**
What do you call this?	**Как это называется?**	kahk **eh**tah nahzi**vah**yeetsah
What do you call that?	**Как это называется?**	kahk **eh**tah nahzi**vah**yeetsah
What does this mean?	**Что это значит?**	shto **eh**tah **znah**chyeet
What does that mean?	**Что это значит?**	shto **eh**tah **znah**chyeet

Do you speak ...?

Do you speak English?	**Вы говорите по-английски?**	vi gahvah**ree**tyee pah ahn**glee**yskee
Do you speak German?	**Вы говорите по-немецки?**	vi gahvah**ree**tyee pahn nyee**myeht**skee
Do you speak French?	**Вы говорите по-французски?**	vi gahvah**ree**tyee pah frahn**tsoos**kee
Do you speak Spanish?	**Вы говорите по-испански?**	vi gahvah**ree**tyee pah ees**pahns**kee
Do you speak Italian?	**Вы говорите по-итальянски?**	vi gahvah**ree**tyee pah eetahl'**yahns**kee

SOME BASIC EXPRESSIONS

Could you speak more slowly, please?	Пожалуйста, говорите медленнее.	pah**zhah**loostah gahvah**ree**tyee **myeh**dlyeenyehyeh
Please point to the phrase in the book.	Покажите мне, пожалуйста, эту фразу в книге.	pahkah**zhi**tyee mnyeh pah**zhah**loostah **eh**too **frah**zoo v **knee**ghyee
Just a minute. I'll see if I can find it in this book.	Сейчас. Я посмотрю, смогу ли я её найти в книжке.	seech**yahss**. yah pahsmah**tryoo** smah**goo** lee yah yee**yo** night**yee** v **knee**zhkyee
I understand.	Я понимаю.	**yah** pahnyeemah**yoo**
I don't understand.	Я не понимаю.	**yah** nyee pahnyeemah**yoo**

Can ...?

Can I have ...?	Можно...?	**mozh**nah
Can we have ...?	Можно...?	**mozh**nah
Can you show me ...?	Вы мне можете показать...?	vi mnyeh **mozh**ityee pahkah**zaht'**
Can you tell me ...?	Вы мне можете сказать...?	vi mnyeh **mozh**ityee skah**zaht'**
Can you help me, please?	Помогите мне, пожалуйста.	pahmah**gyee**tyee mnyeh pah**zhah**loostah

Wanting

I'd like ...	Я хотел бы...	yah khah**tyehl** bi
We'd like ...	Мы хотели бы...	mi khah**tyeh**lee bi
Please give me ...	Дайте мне, пожалуйста,...	**digh**tyee mnyeh pah**zhah**loostah
Give it to me, please.	Дайте мне это, пожалуйста.	**digh**tyee mnyeh **eh**tah pah**zhah**loostah

Please bring me …	**Принесите мне, пожалуйста…**	preenyee**see**tyee mnyeh pah**zhah**loostah
Bring it to me, please.	**Принесите мне это, пожалуйста.**	preenyee**see**tyee mnyeh **eh**tah pah**zhah**loostah
I'm hungry.	**Я голоден.**	**yah go**lahdyeen
I'm thirsty.	**Мне хочется пить.**	mnyeh **kho**chyeetsah peet'
I'm tired.	**Я устал.**	yah oo**stahl**
I'm lost.	**Я заблудился.**	yah zahblood**yeel**sah
It's important.	**Это важно.**	**eh**tah **vahzh**nah
It's urgent.	**Это срочно.**	**eh**tah **sroch'**nah
Hurry up!	**Скорее!**	skah**ryeh**yeh

It is/There is …

The words "it is/there is" are often dropped in Russian. For example, the word холодно (**kho**lahdnah) alone conveys the idea "It is cold".

It is/It's …	**Это…**	**eh**tah
Is it …?	**Это…?**	**eh**tah
It isn't …	**Это не…**	**eh**tah nyeh
There is/There are …	**Есть…**	yehst'
Is there/Are there …?	**Есть ли…?**	yehst' lyee
There isn't/There aren't …	**Нет…**	nyeht
There isn't any/There aren't any.	**Нет.**	nyeht

A few common words

big/small	**большой/маленький**	bahl'**shoy**/**mah**lyeen'keey
quick/slow	**быстро/медленно**	bistrah/**myehd**lyeenah
early/late	**рано/поздно**	rahnah/**poz**nah
cheap/expensive	**дёшево/дорого**	dyoshivah/**do**rahgah
near/far	**близко/далеко**	bleeskah/dahlyee**ko**
hot/cold	**горячо/холодно**	gahryee**chyo**/**kho**lahdnah
full/empty	**полный/пустой**	polniy/poos**toy**
easy/difficult	**легко/трудно**	lyeekh**ko**/**trood**nah
heavy/light	**тяжёлый/легкий**	tyeezholiy/**lyokh**keey
open/shut	**открыто/закрыто**	ahtkritah/zahkritah
right/wrong	**верно/неверно**	vyehrnah/nyeevyehrnah
old/new	**старый/новый**	stahriy/noviy
old/young	**старый/молодой**	stahriy/mahlah**doy**
beautiful/ugly	**красиво/некрасиво**	krahsseevah/nyeekrahsseevah
good/bad	**хорошо/плохо**	khahrah**sho**/**plo**khah
better/worse	**лучше/хуже**	**loo**chshi/**khoo**zhi

A few prepositions and some more useful words

at	**в**	v
on	**на**	nah
in	**в**	v
to	**к**	k
from	**от**	ot
inside	**внутри**	vnoo**tree**
outside	**снаружи**	snah**roo**zhi
up	**вверх**	vvyehrkh
down	**вниз**	vneess
before	**до**	do
after	**после**	pos**lyee**

with	**с**	s
without	**без**	byehss
through	**через**	**chyeh**ryeess
towards	**к**	k
until	**до**	do
during	**во время**	vah **vryeh**myah
and	**и**	ee
or	**или**	**ee**lee
not	**не**	nyeh
nothing	**ничего**	neechyee**vo**
none	**ни один**	nyee ah**deen**
very	**очень**	**o**chyeen'
also	**тоже**	**to**zhi
soon	**скоро**	**sko**rah
perhaps	**может быть**	**mo**zhit bit'
here	**здесь**	zdyehs'
there	**там**	tahm
now	**теперь**	tyee**pyehr'**
then	**тогда**	tahg**dah**

A very basic grammar

Here is the briefest possible outline of some essential features of Russian grammar.

Genders

There are three genders in Russian: masculine, feminine and neuter. There are no preceding articles which could help you identifying them. You must solve the problem from the other end—actually, look at the endings of the words. Here are some basic rules of classification.

Masculine nouns

1. Ending in a hard consonant:

стол	table	мальчик	boy
глаз	eye	стул	chair

2. Ending in a soft consonant:

учитель	teacher

3. Ending in **-й, -ж, -ч, -ш, -щ**:

нож	knife

All these take different forms in the plural. Most often you'll find **-и** and **-ы,** but also **-а, -я** and **-ья.**

ножи	knives	глаза	eyes
столы	tables	учителя	teachers
		стулья	chairs

Feminine nouns

1. Ending in **-я** (after a soft consonant):

неделя	week

2. Ending in **-a** (after a hard consonant):

    книга   book

3. Ending in **-ь**:

    дверь   door

Feminine nouns mostly form their plurals by substituting the last letter of the nominative case by **-и**:

    недели weeks   **книги** books   **двери** doors

Neuter nouns

1. Ending in **-o**:

    окно   window   **яблоко** apple

    The plural is formed by changing the **-o** into **-a**:

    окна   windows

    or into **-и**:

    яблоки   apples

2. Ending in **-e**:

    поле   field

    The plural is formed by changing the **-e** into **-я**:

    поля   fields

Those six cases ...

That's something which presents an obstacle to many enthusiastic hopes of mastering Russian. But don't shy away from it for that obstacle can be easily hurdled. There are six cases in Russian. We'll take them one by one and see how they're used.

The nominative answers the question **кто** (who?) or **что** (what?):

    The girl smiles.   **Девушка улыбается.**

GRAMMAR

The genitive is used to designate a person to whom, or an object to which, somebody or something belongs or refers:

the smile of the girl   **улыбка девушки**

The dative designates the person to whom something is given or done or the object to which something is given or done:

I give it to the girl.   **Я даю это девушке.**

The accusative usually denotes the direct object of an action:

I love that girl.   **Я люблю эту девушку.**

The instrumental is mostly used to denote means by which something is done, or the person by whom something is done:

This story has been written by   **Этот рассказ написан**
the girl.   **девушкой.**

The prepositional is mostly used when you define somebody or something or the place where something is located. Therefore it is also called, in English, the locative case.

We're speaking about the girl.   **Мы говорим о девушке.**

Adjectives

Adjectives agree in number and gender with the noun they modify.

In the masculine nominative form, they usually end in **-ый, -ой,** or **-ий.**

In the feminine nominative form, they usually end in **-ая** or **-яя.**

In the neuter nominative form, they usually end in **-ое** or **-ее.**

And now we're far enough along to give you an example of the declension of the three genders.

	Masculine (quiet evening)	Feminine (shy girl)	Neuter (lucky number)
Singular			
Nom.	тихий вечер	робкая девушка	счастливое число
Gen.	тихого вечера	робкой девушки	счастливого числа
Dat.	тихому вечеру	робкой девушке	счастливому числу
Acc.	тихий вечер	робкую девушку	счастливое число
Inst.	тихим вечером	робкой девушкой	счастливым числом
Prep.	(о)тихом вечере	робкой девушке	счастливом числе
Plural			
Nom.	тихие вечера	робкие девушки	счастливые числа
Gen.	тихих вечеров	робких девушек	счастливых чисел
Dat.	тихим вечерам	робким девушкам	счастливым числам
Acc.	тихие вечера	робких девушек	счастливые числа
Inst.	тихими вечерами	робкими девушками	счастливыми числами
Prep.	(о)тихих вечерах	робких девушках	счастливых числах

Demonstrative pronouns

	Masculine	Feminine	Neuter	Plural
this	этот	эта	это	эти
that	тот	та	то	те

Possessive pronouns

	Masculine	Feminine	Neuter	Plural
my	мой	моя	моё	мои
your	твой	твоя	твоё	твои
his/its	его	его	его	их
her	её	её	её	их
our	наш	наша	наше	наши
your	ваш	ваша	ваше	ваши
their	их	их	их	их

Verbs

The infinitive of most verbs ends in **-ть** or **-ться**. There is also a group of infinitives ending in **-ти**; the most important of these is **идти** (to go).

Given below are the conjugations in the present tense of three verbs:

	брать (to take)	**давать** (to give)	**идти** (to go)
я	беру	даю	иду
ты	берёшь	даёшь	идёшь
он/она/оно	берёт	даёт	идёт
мы	берём	даём	идём
вы/Вы	берёте	даёте	идёте
они	берут	дают	идут

The negative forms of verbs are formed with **не.** Simply "no" in Russian is **нет.**

> He didn't come.   **Он не пришёл.**

Note: There are two forms for "you" in Russian: **ты** (plural: **вы**) is used when talking to relatives, close friends and children, and between young people; **Вы** is used in all other cases. **Вы** is written with a capital **В.**

Arrival

You've arrived. Whether you've come by ship, train or plane, you have to go through passport and customs formalities. (For car-border control, see page 145.)

There's certain to be somebody around who speaks English. That's why we're making this a brief section. What you want is to be off to your hotel or on your way in the shortest possible time. Here are the stages for a speedy departure.

Passport Control

Your travel agent helped you obtain a visa. This is a little booklet that goes with your passport. You must present your passport to the customs officer (often a soldier) who will tear off half of your visa. When you give him your passport, you may want to say:

Here it is.	Пожалуйста.	pah**zhah**loostah
I'll be staying…	Я пробуду здесь…	yah prah**boo**doo zdyehs'
a few days	несколько дней	**nyeh**skahl'kah dnyay
a week	неделю	nyee**dyeh**lyoo
two weeks	две недели	dvyeh nyee**dyeh**lee
a month	месяц	**myeh**sseets
I don't know yet.	Я ещё не знаю.	yah yee**shchyo** nyee **znah**yoo
I'm just passing through.	Я только проездом.	yah **tol'**kah prah**yehz**dahm

If things become difficult:

I'm sorry. I don't understand. Is there anyone here who speaks English?	Простите, я не понимаю. Говорит здесь кто-нибудь по-английски?	prah**stee**tyee yah nyee pahnyee**mah**yoo. gahvah-**reet** zdyehs' **kto**nyeebood' pah ahn**gleey**skee

Customs

When going through customs, don't fail to declare your foreign currency or any precious metals or stones. In this way, you'll be able to take out any unused foreign currency or declared articles when you leave the USSR. There's no limit placed on the amount of foreign currency allowed into the country; on the other hand, no Soviet money may be brought in or taken out.

Note: When changing your money for rubles, don't forget to ask for a receipt or have a note made on your declaration.

The chart below shows you what you can bring in duty-free.*

Cigarettes	Cigars	Tobacco	Liquor (spirits)	Wine
250 or	250 or grams	250 grams	1 and	2

Remember that photographs and printed matter which might be directed against the USSR are prohibited.

I have...	У меня...	oo myeenyah
a carton of cigarettes	блок сигарет	blok seegahryeht
a bottle of whisky	бутылка виски	bootilkah veeskee
a bottle of wine	бутылка вина	bootilkah veenah
100 dollars	100 долларов	100 dollahrahv
50 pounds	50 фунтов	50 foontahv
May I bring this in?	Можно это провезти?	mozhnah ehtah prahveeztee
Here's my declaration form.	Вот моя декларация.	vot mahyah dyeeklahrahtsiyah
I'd like a declaration form in English.	Будьте добры, бланк декларации по-английски.	boottyee dahbri blahnk dyeeklahrahtsiyee pah ahngleeyskee

* All allowances subject to change without notice.

Вы должны заплатить пошлину.	You'll have to pay duty on this.
Платить можете там, в конторе.	Please pay at the office over there.
Есть ли у вас еще багаж?	Have you any more luggage?

Baggage—Porters

Your comprehensive travel arrangements cover the services of a porter and a taxi to your hotel. The fellow with the clipboard—the man from Intourist—will give instructions to the porter. But the following phrases still may be useful.

Porter!	Носильщик!	nah**sseel**'shchyeek
Take my luggage, please.	Пожалуйста, возьмите мой багаж.	pah**zhah**loostah vahz'-**mee**tyee moy bah**gahzh**
I'll hang on to this one/these.	Этот/эти я возьму сам.	**eh**taht/**eh**tyee yah vahz'-**moo** sahm
That... one.	Этот...	**eh**tah
big/small blue/black	большой/маленький синий/черный	bahl'**shoy**/**mah**lyeen'keey **seen**eey/**chyor**niy
There's one piece missing.	Одного места не хватает.	ahdnah**voh** **myeh**stah nyee khvah**tah**yeet
I can't find my porter.	Я не вижу моего носильщика.	yah nyee **vee**zhoo mahyee**vo** nah**ssel**'shchyeekah
Take these bags to the...	Возьмите эти вещи и отнесите к...	vahz'**mee**tyee **eh**tyee **vyeh**shchyee ee ahtnyee**ssee**tyee k
taxi/bus/luggage lockers	такси/автобусу/камере хранения	tahk**see**/ahv**to**boossoo/**kah**myeeryeh khrah-**nyeh**nyeeyah
How much is that?	Сколько я Вам должен?	**skol**'kah yah vahm **dol**zhin
Thank you.	Спасибо.	'spah**ssee**bah

Changing money

You'll find a bank at most airports. If you've come in on a late-afternoon or evening flight and don't have Intourist vouchers for supper, it might be best to change some of your money to rubles before leaving the airport.

Full details about money and currency exchange are given on pages 134–136.

Can you change a traveller's cheque (check)?	Можете ли вы разменять дорожные чеки?	mozhityee lee vi rahzmyee**nyaht'** dah**rozh**niyeh **chyeh**kee
I want to change some…	Я хочу разменять…	yah kha**chyoo** rahzmyee**nyaht'**
traveller's cheques	дорожные чеки	dah**rozh**niyeh **chyeh**kee
dollars	доллары	**doll**ahri
pounds	фунты	**foon**ti
Where's the nearest currency exchange?	Где ближайший обмен денег?	gdyeh blyee**zhigh**shiy ahb**myehn dyeh**nyeeg
What's the exchange rate?	Какой валютный курс?	kah**koy** vah**lyoot**niy koors

Directions

How do I get to…?	Как мне добраться до…?	kahk mnyeh dah**brahts**ah do
Is there a bus into town?	Идёт ли автобус в город?	ee**dyot** lee ahv**to**booss v **go**rahd
Where can I get a taxi?	Где мне достать такси?	gdyeh mnyeh dah**staht'** tah**ksee**
Where can I rent a car?	Где мне взять машину напрокат?	gdyeh mnyeh vzyaht' **mah**shinoo nahprah**kaht**

Hotel reservations

You've certainly made arrangements for a hotel room before coming to the Soviet Union. There'll be an Intourist representative waiting for you once you get through customs. He'll assign you to a hotel and will put you in the hands of your taxi or bus

FOR NUMBERS, see page 175

driver. If, by chance, you can't find the Intourist man, go to the Intourist office in the terminal.

| Where's the Intourist office? | Где бюро Интуриста? | gdyeh byooro eentoo-reestah |
| I need hotel accommodation. | Мне нужно место в гостинице. | mnyeh noozhnah myehstah v gahsteeneetsi |

Car rental

Again, it's best to make arrangements in advance whenever possible. You can rent a car through the Intourist service bureau at most airports and terminals. Rental charges must be paid in foreign currency.

I'd like to rent...	Я хотел бы взять напрокат...	yah khahtyehl bi vzyaht' nahprahkaht
a car	машину	mahshinoo
a small car	маленькую машину	mahlyeen'kooyoo mahshinoo
a large car	большую машину	bahl'shooyoo mahshinoo
I would like it for...	на...	nah
a day/four days	день/четыре дня	dyehn'/chyeetiree dnyah
a week/two weeks	неделю/две недели	nyeedyehlyoo/dvyeh nyeedyehlyee
What's the charge per day?	Сколько это стоит в день?	skol'kah ehtah stoeet v dyehn'
What's the charge per week?	Сколько это стоит в неделю?	skol'kah ehtah stoeet v nyeedyehlyoo
Does that include mileage?	Включён ли в эту цену километраж?	vklyoochyon lee v ehtoo tsehnoo keelahmyeetrahzh
Is petrol (gasoline) included?	Включён ли в эту цену бензин?	vklyoochyon lee v ehtoo tsehnoo byeenzeen
Does that include full insurance?	Включена ли в эту цену страховка?	vklyoochyeenah lee v ehtoo tsehnoo strahkhovkah
What's the deposit?	Какой залог?	kahkoy zahlog
I have a credit card.	У меня есть кредитная карточка.	oo myeenyah yehst' kryehdyeetnahyah kahrtahch'kah

ARRIVAL

FOR SIGHTSEEING, see page 75

Note: Foreigners planning to drive in the Soviet Union must either have an international driving permit or have a Russian translation made of their own licence and attach it to the latter.

Taxis

There's an acute shortage of taxis in the USSR. If you see one, hail it quickly. Taxis may be available at taxi stands. A cab has a checkered line on the door and a green light on the windscreen (windshield). If the light is on, the taxi has no passengers. If you can't get a taxi on the street have someone who speaks Russian phone for one (you can book it a couple of hours in advance). All taxis have meters. You pay according to what the meter reads no matter how many passengers there are.

Where can I get a taxi?	Где можно найти такси?	gdyeh mozhnah nightyee tahksee
Get me a taxi, please.	Найдите мне такси, пожалуйста.	nighdyeetyee mnyeh tahksee pahzhahloostah
What's the fare to…?	Сколько стоит доехать до…?	skol'kah stoeet dahyehkhaht' dah
How far is it to…?	Какое расстояние до…?	kahkoyeh rahsstahyahn'yeh dah
Take me to…	Мне нужно…	mnyeh noozhnah
this address	по этому адресу	po ehtahmoo ahdryeessoo
the centre of town	в центр города	v tsehntr gorahdah
the … Hotel	к гостинице…	k gahsteenyeetseh
Turn left (right) at the next corner.	Поверните налево (направо) за угол.	pahvyeernyeetyee nahlyehvah (nahprahvah) zahoogahl
Go straight ahead.	Прямо.	pryahmah
Stop here, please.	Остановитесь здесь, пожалуйста.	ahstahnahveetyees' zdyehs' pahzhahloostah
I'm in a hurry.	Я спешу.	yah spyeeshoo
There's no hurry.	Я не спешу.	yah nyee spyeeshoo

Hotel—Other accommodation

You must make hotel arrangements before leaving your own country. The USSR issues visas only after hotel reservations have been confirmed. All accommodation must be paid for in advance. Make bookings through a travel agency that cooperates with Intourist (the state travel agency) or Sovincentr (an agency operating hotels geared to the businessman). While you're free to request the hotel of your choice, the final arrangements rest with Intourist or Sovincentr, who let you know the decision on arrival at the airport.

Hotel accommodation is divided into three categories:

deluxe	suite with bath
first class	single or double room with bath
tourist	two- or three-bed room without bath

If you're travelling on your own, you'll hardly be able to get tourist-class accommodation since it's reserved for group tours.

If you drive a car, you may also arrange to stay at camping sites. In addition, there are inexpensive two-week study trips set up by USSR friendship organizations in various countries.

Note: You may have trouble finding a single room in Moscow, Leningrad and Kiev during the periods of July-August, around May 1 (Labour Day) and November 7 and 8 (October Revolution Days).

In the next few pages we consider your requirements—step by step—from arrival to departure. You need not read through all of it; just turn to the situation that applies.

HOTEL

Checking in—Reception

My name is...	**Меня зовут...**	myee**nyah** zah**voot**
I've a reservation.	**Я заказал заранее.**	yah zahkah**zahl** zah**rah**-n'yeh
We've reserved two rooms, a single and a double.	**Мы заказали два номера, одинарный и двойной.**	mi zahkah**zahl**yee dvah **no**myeerah ahdyee**nahr**niy ee dvigh**noy**
I'd like...	**Я хотел бы...**	yah khah**tyehl** bi
a single room	**одинарный номер**	ahdyee**nahr**niy **no**myeer
a double room	**двойной номер**	dvigh**noy no**myeer
two single rooms	**два одинарных номера**	dvah ahdyee**nahr**nikh **no**myeerah
a room with twin beds	**номер с двуспальной кроватью**	**no**myeer s dvoo**spahl'**nigh krah**vaht'**yoo
a room with a bath	**номер с ванной**	**no**myeer s **vahn**nigh
a room with a shower	**номер с душем**	**no**myeer s **doo**shehm
a room with a balcony	**номер с балконом**	**no**myeer s bahl**ko**nahm
a room with a view	**номер с видом**	**no**myeer s **vyee**dahm
We'd like a room...	**Мы хотели бы номер...**	mi khah**tyehl**yee bi **no**myeer
in the front	**на передней стороне**	nah pyee**ryehd**nyay stah**rah**nyeh
facing the sea	**с окнами на море**	s **ok**nahmyee **nah** moryeh
facing the courtyard	**с окнами во двор**	s **ok**nahmyee vah dvor
It must be quiet.	**Номер нужен тихий.**	**no**myeer **noo**zhin **tyee**khyeey
I'd rather have something higher up (lower down).	**Я хотел бы этажом повыше (пониже).**	yah khah**tyehl** bi ehtah**zhom** pah**vi**sheh (pah**nyee**zheh)
Is there...?	**Есть ли...?**	yehst' lyee
air conditioning/ heating	**кондиционер/ отопление**	kahndyeetsiah**nyehr** ahtah**plyehn**'yeh
a radio/television in the room	**радио/телевизор в номере**	**rah**dyeeo/tyehlyeh**vee**zahr v **no**myeeryeh
hot water	**горячая вода**	gah**ryah**chyeeyah vah**dah**
a private toilet	**свой туалет**	svoy tooah**lyeht**

How much?

What's the price...?	Сколько стоит номер...?	skol'kah stoeet nomyeer
per week	в неделю	v nyeedyehlyoo
per night	в сутки	v sootkee
for bed and breakfast	с завтраком	s zahvtrahkahm
excluding meals	без питания	byehz pyeetahn'yah
for full board	с полным содержанием	s polnim sahdyeerzhahn'yehm
Does that include...?	Включён ли...	vklyoochyon lyee
breakfast	завтрак	zahvtrahk
meals	питание	pyeetahn'yeh
service	обслуживание	ahbsloozhivahn'yeh
Is there any reduction for children?	Для детей нет скидки?	dlyah dyeetyay nyeht skeedkee
Do you charge for the baby?	За ребёнка платить особо?	zah ryeebyonkah plahtyeet' ahssobah
That's too expensive.	Это слишком дорого.	ehtah sleeshkahm dorahgah
Haven't you anything cheaper?	Есть ли у вас что-нибудь подешевле?	yehst' lyee oo vahss shtonyeebood' pahdyeeshehvlyee

How long?

We'll be staying...	Мы пробудем здесь...	mi prahboodyeem zdyehs'
overnight only	только сутки	tol'kah sootkee
a few days	несколько дней	nyehskahl'kah dnyay
a week (at least)	неделю (по крайней мере)	nyeedyehlyoo (pah krighnyeey myehryeh)
I don't know yet.	Я ещё не знаю.	yah yeeshchyo nyee znahyoo

FOR NUMBERS, see page 175

HOTEL

Decision

May I see the room?	Можно посмотреть номер?	mozhnah pahsmahtryeht' nomyeer
No, I don't like it.	Нет, мне не нравится.	nyeht mnyeh nyee nrahveetsah
It's too…	Здесь слишком…	zdyehs' slyeeshkahm
cold/hot	холодно/жарко	kholahdnah/zhahrkah
dark/small	темно/тесно	tyeemno/tyehsnah
noisy	шумно	shoomnah
No, that won't do at all.	Нет, это никак не подходит.	nyeht ehtah nyeekahk nyee pahdkhodyeet
I asked for a room with a bath.	Я просил номер с ванной.	yah prahsseel nomyeer s vahnnigh
Have you anything…?	Есть ли у вас что-нибудь…?	yehst' lyee oo vahss shto-nyeebood'
better/bigger	получше/побольше	pahloochsheh/pahbol'sheh
cheaper/smaller	подешевле/поменьше	pahdyeeshehvlyee/pahmyehn'sheh
Have you a room with a better view?	Есть ли у вас номер с лучшим видом?	yehst' lyee oo vahss nomyeer s loochshim veedahm
That's fine. I'll take it.	Хорошо. Это подойдёт.	khahrahsho. ehtah pahdighdyot

HOTEL

Tipping

A service charge is normally included in your bill. While tipping is officially frowned upon in the USSR, Western guests may show their appreciation for good service by leaving a little extra on the table. Chambermaids do not expect tips, but will be pleased to receive chocolate, cigarettes or nylon stockings.

FOR TIPPING, see also page 1

Registration

Upon arrival at a hotel you'll be asked to fill in a registration form (регистрационный лист— ryehgeestrahtsi**on**niy leest). It asks your name, home address, passport number and further destination. It's almost certain to carry an English translation. If it doesn't, ask the desk-clerk:

What does this mean?	**Что это значит?**	shto **eh**tah **znah**chyeet

The desk-clerk will ask you for your passport. He'll want to keep it overnight. Don't worry, you'll get it back. The desk-clerk may want to say to you:

Ваш паспорт, пожалуйста.	May I see your passport?
Будьте добры заполнить регистрационный лист.	Would you mind filling in this registration form?
Подпишитесь тут, пожалуйста.	Sign here, please.
Как долго вы здесь пробудете?	How long will you be staying?

What's my room number?	**Какой мой номер?**	kah**koy** moy **no**myeer
Will you have our bags sent up?	**Отправьте, пожалуйста, наш багаж в номер.**	aht**prahv**tyee pah**zhah**loostah nahsh bah**gahzh** v **no**myeer
I'll take this briefcase with me.	**Этот портфель я возьму с собой.**	**eh**taht pahrt**fyehl'** yah vahz'**moo** s sah**boy**

Service, please

Now that you are safely installed, meet some more of the staff:

the maid	горничная	**g**ornyeeshnahyah
the floor manager	дежурная	dyeezhoornahyah
the manager	администратор	ahdmyeenyee**s**trahtahr
the telephone operator	телефонистка	tyeelyeefahn**yees**tkah

When speaking to members of the staff, use a general introductory phrase such as:

Excuse me. Could you .... please?	Извините, нельзя ли...?	eezveen**yee**tyee nyeel'**zyah** lyee

General requirements

Please ask the maid to come up.	Пришлите, пожалуй-ста, горничную.	pree**shlee**tyee pahzhahloo-stah **g**ornyeeshnooyoo
Who is it?	Кто там?	kto tahm
Come in!	Войдите!	vigh**dyee**tyee
Is there a bath on this floor?	Есть ли на этаже ванная комната?	yehst' lyee nah ehtah**zheh vahn**nahyah **kom**nahtah
Where's the plug for the razor?	Где розетка для бритвы?	gdyeh rah**zyeht**kah dlyah **breet**vi
What's the voltage?	Какое здесь напря-жение?	kah**koy**eh zdyehs' nahpryah-**zhehn'**yeh
Please send up...	Пришлите, пожалуй-ста...	pree**shlee**tyee pahzhah-**loo**stah
two coffees	две чашки кофе	dvyeh **chahshk**ee **kof**yeh
a sandwich	бутерброд	bootyeer**brod**
two vodkas and soda	две рюмки водки и минеральную воду	dvyeh **ryoom**kee **vod**kee ee meenyee**rahl'**nooyoo **vod**oo
Can we have break-fast in our room?	Можно получить зав-трак в номер?	**mozh**nah pahlooch**yeet' zahv**trahk v **nom**yeer
I'd like to leave these in your safe.	Я хотел бы оставить это у вас в сейфе.	yah khah**tyehl** bi ah**stah**veet' **eh**tah oo vahss v **syay**fyee

May I have a/an/some...?	Принесите мне, пожалуйста...	preenyeesseetyee mnyeh pahzhahloostah
ashtray	пепельницу	pyehpyeel'nyeetsoo
bath towel	банное полотенце	bahnnahyeh pahlah-tyehntseh
extra blanket	ещё одно одеяло	yeeshchyo ahdno ahdyee-yahlah
envelopes	конверты	kahnvyehrti
hot-water bottle	грелку	gryehlkoo
ice	льда	l'dah
needle and thread	иголку с ниткой	eegolkoo s nyeetkigh
extra pillow	ещё одну подушку	yeeshchyo ahdnoo pahdooshkoo
reading-lamp	настольную лампу	nahstol'nooyoo lahmpoo
soap	мыло	milah
writing-paper	бумагу для писем	boomahgoo dlyah pyeesseem
Where's the...?	Где...?	gdyeh
bathroom	ванная	vahnnahyah
beauty salon	косметический кабинет	kahs'myeetyeechyeeskeey kahbeenyeht
cocktail lounge	бар	bahr
dining room	столовая	stahlovahyah
hairdresser's	парикмахерская	pahreekmahkhyehrskahyah
restaurant	ресторан	ryeestahrahn
television room	телевизор	tyehlyehveezahr
toilet	туалет	tooahlyeht

> **ЗВОНОК**
> RING FOR SERVICE

Breakfast

The Russian breakfast can be quite hearty. Besides the usual fare of tea or coffee with bread, butter and jam, a Russian might have ham and eggs, cheese, cereals, sausages or cold cuts. This might be all washed down with a glass of vodka. So in the Soviet Union you'll be able to tailor your breakfast menu to suit your own morning appetite.

I'll have a/an/some…	Дайте мне, пожалуйста…	dightyee mnyeh pahzhahloostah
ham and eggs	яичницу с ветчиной	yeeeeeshnyeetsoo s veechyeenoy
hot cereal	каши	kahshi
eggs	яйца	yightsah
boiled egg	варёные яйца	vahryoniyeh yightsah
soft/medium/hard	всмятку/в мешочек/крутые	vsmyahtkoo/v meeshochyeek/krootiyeh
fried	яичницу	yeeeeeshnyeetsoo
scrambled	яйца всмятку	yightsah vsmyahtkoo
fruit juice	фруктовый сок	frooktoviy sok
grapefruit	грейпфрутовый	graypfrootahviy
orange	апельсиновый	ahpyeel'seenahviy
pineapple	ананасый	ahnahnahsniy
tomato	томатный	tahmahtniy
kidneys	почек	poch'kyee
liver	печень	pyehchyehn'
omelet	омлет	ahmlyeht
sausages	сосиски	sahsseeskyee
May I have some…?	Дайте мне, пожалуйста…	dightyee mnyeh pahzhahloostah
hot/cold milk	теплого/холодного молока	tyoplahvah/khahlodnahvah mahlahkah
cream/sugar	сливки/сахар	slyeevkee/sahkhahr
more butter	ещё масла	yeeshchyo mahslah
salt/pepper	соль/перец	sol'/pyehryehts
coffee/tea	кофе/чаю	kofyeh/chahyoo
cocoa	какао	kahkaho
lemon/honey	лимон/мёд	leemon/myod
Could you bring me a…?	Принесите мне, пожалуйста…	preenyeesseetye mnyeh pahzhahloostah
plate	тарелку	tahryehlkoo
glass	стакан	stahkahn
cup	чашку	chyahshkoo
knife	нож	nozh
fork	вилку	veelkoo
spoon	ложку	lozhkoo

HOTEL SERVICE

Note: You'll find a great many other dishes listed in our guide "Eating Out" (pages 38–64). This should be consulted for your lunch and dinner menus.

Difficulties

The ... doesn't work.	...не действует.	... nyee **dyay**stvooyeet
air-conditioner	кондиционер	kahndyeetsiah**nyehr**
fan	вентилятор	vyeentyee**lyah**tahr
heating	отопление	ahtah**plyeh**nyeh
tap (faucet)	водопроводный кран	vahdahprah**vod**niy krahn
toilet	туалет	tooah**lyeht**
The light doesn't work.	Не горит свет.	nyee gah**reet** svyeht
The wash-basin is clogged.	Раковина засорена.	**rah**kahveenah sahssah**ree**nah
The window is jammed.	Окно испорчено.	ahk**no** eespor**chyee**nah
The blind is stuck.	Шторы не ходят.	**shto**ri nyee **kho**dyaht
This isn't my laundry.	Это не моё бельё.	**eh**tah nyee mah**yo** byeel'**yo**
There's no hot water.	Нет горячей воды.	nyeht gah**ryah**chyay vah**di**
I've lost my watch.	Я потерял часы.	yah pahtyee**ryahl** chyee**ssi**
I've left my key in my room.	Я забыл ключ в номере.	yah zah**bil** klyooch' v **no**myeeryee
The ... is broken.	...сломана/сломано.	... **slo**mahnah/**slo**mahno
lamp	лампа	**lahm**pah
plug	штепсель	**shtehp**syehl'
shutter	жалюзи	zhah**lyoo**zee
switch	выключатель	vik**lyoo**chyah**tyehl'**
window shade	шторы	**shto**ri
The bulb is burnt out.	Лампочка перегорела.	**lahm**pahch'kah pyeeree-gah**ryeh**lah

Telephone—Mail—Callers

I want to make a local call.	Город, пожалуйста.	**go**rahd pah**zhah**loostah
Can you get me Moscow 123-45-67?	Соедините меня, пожалуйста, с Москвой, номер 123-45-67.	sahyehd**yee**nyeetyee myee**nyah** pah**zhah**loostah s mah**skvoy** **no**myeer 123-45-67
Did anyone telephone me?	Никто мне не звонил?	nyee**kto** mnyeh nyee zvah**nyeel**

FOR POST OFFICE, see page 137

Is there any mail for me?	Для меня писем нет?	dlyah myee**nyah** pees**seem** nyeht
Have you any stamps?	Есть ли у вас почто-вые марки?	yehst' lyee oo vahss pahch'-**to**viyeh **mahr**kee
Would you mail this for me, please?	Отправьте, пожа-луйста.	aht**prahv**tyee pah**zhah**-loostah

Checking out

I'm leaving early tomorrow.	Я уезжаю завтра рано утром.	yah ooyeezh**zhah**yoo **zahv**-trah **rah**nah **oo**trahm
I've got to leave at once.	Я должен немедлен-но уехать.	yah **dol**zhin nyee**myehd**-lyeennah oo**yehk**khaht'
Can you arrange to have a taxi here at…?	Закажите мне, пожа-луйста, такси к …?	zahkah**zhi**tyee mnyeh pah-**zhah**loostah tahk**see** k
When's the next…?	В котором часу от-ходит следующий…?	v kah**to**rahm chyee**sso**o aht**kho**dyeet **slyehd**ooy-shchyeey
bus	автобус	ahv**to**booss
train	поезд	**po**eezd
plane	самолёт (отлетает)	sahmah**lyot** (ahtlyee**ta**heet)
Will you have some-one bring my bags down?	Пришлите, пожалуй-ста, снести мои чемоданы.	pryee**shlyee**tyee pah**zhah**-loostah snyee**stee** mahee chyeemah**dah**nee
Please let me know when the taxi comes.	Дайте мне знать, пожалуйста, когда подъедет такси.	**dight**yee mnyeh znaht' pah**zhah**loostah kahg**dah** pahd'**yeh**dyeet tahk**see**
Is that our taxi?	Это наше такси?	**eh**tah **nah**sheh tahk**see**
Here's my forward-ing address. You've got my home address.	Вот мой следующий адрес. Мой домашний адрес у вас уже есть.	vot moy **slyehd**ooyshchyeey **ahd**ryehss. moy dah**mash**-nyeey **ahd**ryehss oo vahss oo**zheh** yest'
It's been a very enjoyable stay.	Всё было очень при-ятно.	vsyo **bi**lah **o**chyehn' pryee-**yaht**nah
We hope to come again some day.	Может быть, мы приедем ещё.	**mo**zheht bit' mi pree**yeh**-dyehm yee**shchyo**
Good-bye.	До свидания.	dah svee**dah**n'yah

HOTEL SERVICE

FOR TAXI, see page 27

Eating out

There are many types of places where you can eat and drink in the Soviet Union. Most eating places display a menu in the window or at the door.

Бар (bahr)	Bar. Many hotels in big cities and well-known resorts have bars that serve all kinds of drinks along with caviar and crabmeat (usually foreign currency must be used). They generally close at 2 or 3 a.m.
Буфет (boo**fyeht**)	Snack bar, found in every hotel. It's often located in an obscure corner on an upper floor of the hotel.
Диетическая столовая (dyeeeh**tyee**chyehs-kahyah stah**lo**vahyah)	Health-food restaurant. Dietetic meals at fairly low prices
Кафе (kah**feh**)	Café. Despite its name, a Russian *café* actually comes closer to being the equivalent of our restaurant. Found everywhere these places serve meals and drinks until 9 p.m.; a few remain open till 11 p.m.
Кафе-мороженое (kah**feh** mahrozheh-nahyeh)	Ice-cream parlour. You can get both ice-cream and drinks (mostly champagne and cocktails)
Пельменная (pyeel′**myehn**nahyah)	Small eating places, mainly serving stuffed dumplings and a few other dishes
Пивной бар (peev**noy** bahr)	Beer halls where some appetizers, such as shrimp, can be found

Пирожковая
(peerahzhkovahyah)

Another speciality place that sells nothing but *pirozhok*: small turnovers with savoury fillings

Ресторан
(ryeestahrahn)

The Russians have adapted *restaurant* to their language. But in most cases it actually means a dinner-and-dance restaurant. Between courses, Russians might down a glass or two of vodka, tell a few raucous jokes and then have a twirl with their partner on the dance floor. When making your travel arrangements, it's a good idea to pay in advance for breakfast only. This will enable you to eat lunch and supper anywhere you please, i.e., in the types of places listed on these pages where Intourist meal vouchers aren't accepted. However, the vouchers can be used in all Intourist-recognized hotels that have restaurants, as well as in the most famous restaurants. Closing time is usually midnight.

Столовая
(stahlovahyah)

Here's where the ordinary man eats; often cafeteria-style

Шашлычная
(shahslich'nahyah)

Generally crowded cafés where they serve *shashlik* and other typical dishes from the Caucasus and Central Asia

Meal times

Lunch (Обед —ahbyehd): from about noon to 4 p.m. in most restaurants. They close at 5 p.m. and re-open at 7 p.m.

Dinner (Ужин—oozhin): from 7 p.m. to 10 or 10.30 p.m. After that, there are only cold snacks to be had.

FOR BREAKFAST, see page 34

EATING OUT

Eating habits

While the situation is changing very rapidly, the Soviet Union may still be considered the last frontier in travel. There's an exciting strangeness about everything in the USSR, and this is especially true about eating habits. The first surprise is finding oneself faced with a menu written in Cyrillic characters. Then we find such anomalies as the буфет (boo**fyeht**—literally: buffet), where you can purchase food by the gram and litre and consume it at nearby tables. At home, Russians may breakfast heartily on buckwheat porridge with generous pats of butter, or frankfurters and tomatoes, or half a loaf of black bread and a bottle of milk. You'll be surprised by the way they put a scoop of sour cream on everything, or by their fondness for кефир (kyeh**feer**—a type of sour milk sold by the glass or bottle and usually topped off with a great deal of sugar).

While the Anglo-Saxon traveller will find Russian food unlike the standardized fare he's used to, there's no adjustment problem. You can eat almost anything you'd like without a thought about getting an upset stomach. If you're travelling in Central Asia, however, you'll have to be a bit cautious about the drinking water or unwashed vegetables.

Russians seem to hold our genteel table manners in contempt. At home and in neighbourhood restaurants, the atmosphere is most often warm and boisterous as the room rings with hearty laughter, song and lively conversations. The vodka flows freely. You should try to drop in at the corner café to get a glimpse of the local scene.

If you get homesick for good old cellophane-wrapped food served in glass and stainless steel surroundings, visit one of Moscow's modern cafeterias on Kalinin Avenue.

When dining with Russian friends, it is appropriate to wish them приятного аппетита (pree**yaht**nahvah ahpyee**tyee**tah— hearty appetite!).

Hungry?

I'm hungry/	**Я голоден/**	yah **go**lahdyeen/
I'm thirsty.	**Я хочу пить.**	yah khah**chyoo** peet'
Can you recommend a good restaurant?	**Не можете ли порекомендовать, хороший ресторан?**	nyee **mo**zhityee lyee pahryeekahmyeendah**vaht'** khah**ro**shiy ryeesta**rahn**

If you want to be sure of getting a table in well-known restaurants, it may be better to telephone in advance.

Asking and ordering

You'll have to order à la carte in restaurants. Don't forget that a service charge is always included in the prices, though you may want to leave a tip for the waiter if you enjoyed the meal and the service.

Good evening. I'd like a table for three.	**Добрый вечер. Я хотел бы столик на троих.**	**do**briy **vyeh**chyeer. yah khah**tyehl** bi **sto**lyeek nah tra**heekh**
Could we have a...?	**Пожалуйста...**	pah**zhah**loostah
table in the corner	**столик в углу**	**sto**lyeek v oo**gloo**
table by the window	**столик у окна**	**sto**lyeek oo ahk**nah**
table outside	**столик снаружи**	**sto**lyeek snah**roo**zhi
quiet table somewhere	**столик в тихом месте**	**sto**lyeek v **tyee**khahm **myehs**tyee
Where are the toilets?	**Где туалет?**	gdyeh tooah**lyeht**
Could we have a/an...?	**Принесите нам, пожалуйста...**	preenyee**see**tyee nahm pah**zhah**loostah
ashtray	**пепельницу**	**pyeh**pyeel'nyeetsoo
bottle of...	**бутылку...**	boo**til**koo
another chair	**ещё один стул**	yeesh**chyo** ah**dyeen** stool
glass	**стакан**	stah**kahn**
glass of water	**стакан воды**	stah**kahn** vah**di**
knife	**нож**	nozh
napkin	**салфетку**	sahl**fyeht**koo
plate	**тарелку**	tah**ryehl**koo
spoon	**ложку**	**lozh**koo
toothpick	**зубочистку**	zoobah**chyeest**koo
tablecloth	**скатерть**	**skah**tyehrt'

EATING OUT

I'd like a/an/some…	Принесите, пожалуйста…	preenyeessseetye pahzhahloostah
appetizer	закуску	zahkooskoo
beer	пива	peevah
bread	хлеба	khlyehbah
butter	масла	mahslah
cabbage	капусты	kahpoosti
cheese	сыру	siroo
coffee	кофе	kofyeh
dessert	третье	tryeht'yeh
fish	рыбу	riboo
fowl	птицу	ptyeetsoo
french fries	жареной картошки	zhahryeenigh kahrtoshkee
fruit	фруктов	frooktahv
game	дичи	dyeechyee
ice-cream	мороженого	mahrozhinahvah
lemon	лимон	leemon
meat	мясо	myahssah
mineral water	минеральной воды	meenyeerahl'nigh vahdi
milk	молока	mahlahkah
mustard	горчицы	gahrchyeetsi
oil	растительного масла	rahstyeetyeel'nahvah mahslah
olive oil	прованского масла	prahvahnskahvah mahslah
pepper	перцу	pyehrtsoo
potatoes	картошки	kahrtoshkee
rice	рису	reessoo
rolls	булочек	boolahchyehk
salad	салат	sahlaht
salt	соли	solyee
sandwich	бутерброд	booteerbrod
snack	лёгкую закуску	lyokhkooyoo zahkooskoo
soup	супу	soopoo
sugar	сахару	sahkhahroo
tea	чаю	chyahyoo
vegetables	овощей	ahvahshchyay
vinegar	уксусу	ooksoossoo
water	воды	vahdi
wine	вина	veenah

What's on the menu?

Our menu has been presented according to courses. Under each heading you'll find an alphabetical list of dishes in Russian with their English equivalents. This list—which includes everyday items and special dishes—will enable you to make the most of a Russian menu.

Here's our guide to good eating and drinking. Turn to the course you want to start with.

EATING OUT

Obviously, you're not going to go through every course on the menu. If you've had enough, say:

Nothing else, thanks.	**Больше ничего, спасибо.**	**bol**'sheh nyeechyee**vo** spah**ssee**bah

Service in Soviet cafés and restaurants is notoriously on the slow side—sometimes up to two hours to get what you ordered. Don't forget that Russians come to such places to while away the evening—particularly at a dinner-and-dance restaurant. If you're really in a hurry, you might discreetly slip the waiter one ruble and watch the service perk up.

Appetizers

Many a foreigner dining out in the Soviet Union has mistaken the закуски (zah**koos**kee—appetizers) for the main meal. So if you find yourself faced with a huge platter of *hors-d'œuvre*, try to save some room for the entrées. It'd be rather pointless to show up for a dinner if you'd been eating snacks all day.

ветчина	veechyee**nah**	ham
винегрет	veenyee**gryeht**	vegetable salad
грибы	**gree**bi	mushrooms
колбаса	kahlbah**ssah**	cold cuts
копчёная колбаса	kahp**chyo**nahyah kahlbah**ssah**	smoked cold cuts
креветки	kree**veht**kyee	shrimp
мясная закуска	myahs**nah**yah zah**koos**kah	cold cuts
осетрина	ahssyee**tree**nah	sturgeon
редиска	reed**yees**kah	radishes
рыбная закуска	**rib**nahyah zah**koos**kah	assorted fish
салат из крабов	sah**laht** eez **krah**bahv	crabmeat salad
салат из огурцов	sah**laht** eez ah**goorts**ov	cucumber salad
салат из помидоров	sah**laht** eez pah**mee**dorahv	tomato salad
сельдь	**syehl**'d'	herring
студень	**stoo**dyeen'	aspic, e.g., pig's knuckle in aspic
сардины	**sahr**dyeeni	sardines
шпроты	**shpro**ti	sprats
яйца	**yight**sah	eggs
яйца под майонезом	**yight**sah pahd mahyah**neh**zahm	egg salad

Russian specialities

A luxury item in most countries, caviar (икра—ee**krah**) isn't even available to the average Russian nowadays. However, you'll find it offered on the menus of restaurants catering to an international clientele. Red caviar (красная икра—**krahs**nahyah ee**krah**)—about the size of buckshot—is the roe of the salmon. It's salty and cheaper than black caviar which comes from the sturgeon. Caviar is often served in sandwiches (бутерброды — booteer**bro**di) or with pancakes (блины –blyee**ni**) which are smaller and thicker than American or British pancakes and made with yeast.

Other typically Russian appetizers are:

Блины со сметаной	blyeeni sah smeetah-nigh	Russian pancakes filled with sour cream and then baked
Грибы в сметане	greebi v smyeetahnyee	Sliced mushrooms, fried with onions and served with sour cream
Заливная осетрина с хреном	zahlyeevnahyah ahssyee-treenah s khryehnahm	Sturgeon in aspic with horseradish
Икра из баклажанов	eekrah eez bahklahzhah-nahv	"Eggplant caviar"; mashed eggplants, onions, tomatoes
Маринованные грибы	mahreenovahniyeh greebi	Pickled mushrooms
Осетрина с гарниром	ahssyeetreenah s gahr-nyeerahm	Sturgeon with vegetables
Сельдь с луком	syehl'd' s lookahm	Herring with onions
Тресковая печень в масле	treeskovahyah pyehchyeen' v mahslyee	Cod liver in oil

In the Soviet Union, salad and egg dishes fall under the general heading of appetizers. In the same way, cheese has its place at the start of a big meal and isn't eaten after the main course.

Salad appetizers

Винегрет (veenyeegryeht)	Vegetable salad composed of diced carrots, beets, potatoes, mixed in oil and vinegar
Салат из редиса (sahlaht eez reedyeesah)	Finely sliced radishes with sour cream and salt
Салат из свежей капусты (sahlaht eez svyehzhay kahpoosti)	Fresh cabbage, spring onions, apples, mixed with sugar and vegetable oil
Салат московский/ столичный (sahlaht mahskov-skeey/stahleech'niy)	A salad of beef, potatoes, eggs, carrots, apples, mayonnaise, sour cream

Egg appetizers

Крутые яйца с хреном (**kroo**tiee **yight**sah s **khrye**hnahm)	Hard-boiled eggs with horseradish, mayonnaise and sour cream
Яйца с икрой (**yight**sah s ee**kroy**)	Hard-boiled eggs filled with soft caviar and served with lettuce

Cheese and other dairy products

As we've already mentioned, cheese is generally eaten in Russia as an appetizer, at breakfast or as a light snack. A popular type of cheese that you might find is голландский сыр (gah**lahn**skeey syr—Dutch-style cheese). Here are some more dairy products and favourite dairy dishes:

блинчики с творогом (**blyeen**chyeekee s **tvo**rahgom)	Pancakes filled with cottage cheese
вареники с творогом (vah**ryeh**nyeekee s **tvo**rahgom)	Stuffed Ukrainian dumplings
кефир (kee**feer**)	Sour milk
ряженка (**ryah**zhinkah)	Sour baked milk, served chilled
сливки (**slyeev**kee)	Cream
сметана (smee**tah**nah)	Sour cream, an integral part of Russian cooking. It's used in soups, salads, vegetable and meat dishes as well as on desserts.
сырники со сметаной (**sir**nyeekee sah smyee**tah**nigh)	Cheese fritters served with sour cream
творог (**tvo**rog)	A cottage cheese not unlike the American variety. This extremely popular soft cheese is the main ingredient in a number of dishes.
топлёное молоко (tahp**lyo**nahyeh mahlah**ko**)	Baked milk, served chilled

Soups

Most Anglo-Saxons have only heard of one Russian soup: *borsch*. They also have the idea that *borsch* is a cold, red soup invariably served with sour cream. Actually, there are many versions of this soup which is often an entire meal in itself. The word *borsch* comes from the old Slavic word for beets, and the soup is almost certain to be reddish in colour. However, it's usually served hot and may contain cabbage, beef and pork.

Hot soups

борщ московский	borshch' mahs**kov**skeey	beef, vegetables, tomato purée, bacon
борщ флотский	borshch' **flots**keey	bacon or ham bones, vegetables, tomato purée
бульон куриный с гренками	bool'**yon** koor**yee**niy s **gryehn**kahmee	chicken broth with sippets (croutons)
бульон с пирожком	bool'**yon** s peerahzh**kom**	chicken broth with small turnovers
бульон с фрикадельками	bool'**yon** s freekah**dyehl'** kahmee	chicken broth with meat dumplings
рассольник	rahs**sol'**nyeek	kidney and cucumber soup
солянка мясная сборная	**sah**lyahnkah myahs**nah**yah **sbor**nahyah	thick meat soup
солянка рыбная	**sah**lyahnkah **rib**nahyah	thick fish soup
суп-лапша с курицей	soop lahp**shah** s **koo**reetsay	chicken noodle soup
уха	oo**khah**	fish consommé
щи	shchee	cabbage and vegetables
щи зелёные с яйцом	shchee zeel**yo**niyeh s yeet**som**	sorrel soup thickened with a beaten egg
щи суточные	shchee **soo**tach'niyeh	sauerkraut soup

Cold soups

ботвинья с осетриной	baht**veen'**yah s ahsyee-**tree**nigh	vegetables and sturgeon
окрошка мясная сборная	ah**krosh**kah myees**nah**yah **sbor**nahyah	*kvass* soup of assorted meat
свекольник	svyee**kol'**nyeek	beet soup
фруктовый суп	frook**to**viy soop	fruit soup

Oriental soups

пити	peetyee	mutton soup, traditionally prepared in small individual tureens
суп харчо	soop khahrchyo	mutton and rice soup
шурпа	shoorpah	mutton soup with bacon and tomatoes

Fish and seafood

With its thousands of miles of coastline on the Atlantic and Pacific Oceans, as well as those on the Black Sea and Baltic Sea, the Soviet Union ranks among the world's leading fishing nations. Once he's tried caviar, the traveller should make a point of sampling Russian salmon, sturgeon and carp. On the other hand, some common types of shellfish, like lobster or oysters, just aren't found in Russian restaurants.

I'd like some fish.	**Я бы взял рыбы.**	yah bi vzyal ribi
камбала	kahmbahlah	flounder
карп	kahrp	carp
кета	keetah	Siberian salmon
краб	krahb	crab
лещ	lyehshch'	bream
макрель	mahkryehl'	mackerel
минога	meenogah	lamprey
окунь	okoon'	perch
осётр	ahssyotr	sturgeon
палтус	pahltoos	halibut
раки	rahkee	crayfish
сельдь	syehl'd'	herring
сёмга	syomgah	salmon
сом	som	sheatfish (large catfish)
судак	soodahk	pike perch
треска	tryeeskah	cod
тунец	toonyehts	tunny fish, tuna
угорь	oogor'	eel
устрицы	oostreetsi	oysters
форель	fahrehl'	trout
шпроты	shproti	sprats (in oil)
щука	shchyookah	pike

EATING OUT

There are many ways of preparing fish. Here are the Russian translations of the ways you may want it served:

baked	печёный	pyeechyoniy
fried	жареный	zhahryeeniy
deep fried	сильно прожареный	seel'nah prahzhahryeeniy
grilled	жареный на рашпере (вертеле)	zhahryeeniy nah rahsh-pyeeryeh (vyehrtyeelyeh)
marinated	маринованый	mahreenovahniy
poached	отварной	ahtvahrnoy
raw	сырой	siroy
smoked	копчёный	kahpchyoniy
steamed	паровой	pahrahvoy
stewed	тушёный	tooshoniy

Fish specialities

осетрина под маринадом	ahssyeetreenah pahd mahreenahdahm	pickled sturgeon
осетрина в томате	ahssyeetreenah v tahmahtyee	sturgeon in tomato sauce
осетрина на вертеле	ahssyeetreenah nah vyehrtyeelyeh	spit-grilled sturgeon
осетрина по-русски	ahssyeetreenah pah rooskee	poached sturgeon with tomato sauce and vegetables
осетрина паровая	ahssyeetreenah pahrahvahyah	steamed sturgeon served with a light sauce
осетрина «фри»	ahssyeetreenah free	fried sturgeon
палтус жареный	pahltooss zhahryeeniy	fried halibut
рыбные котлеты	ribniyeh kahtlyehti	fish croquettes
стерлядь паровая	styehrlyahd' pahrahvahyah	steamed sterlet
судак в томатном соусе	soodahk v tahmahtnahm sooossyeh	sautéed pike-perch served in tomato sauce
судак отварной, соус яичный	soodahk ahtvahrnoy soooss yeeeeshniy	poached pike-perch in egg sauce
судак «фри»	soodahk free	fried pike-perch

Meat

What kinds of meat have you got?	**Какое у вас есть мясо?**	kahkoyeh oo vahss yest' myahssah
баранина	bahrahnyeenah	mutton
бараньи котлеты	bahrahn'yee kahtlyehti	mutton chops
бекон	byehkon	bacon
битки	beetkee	meatballs
бифштекс	beefshtehks	beefsteak
ветчина	veechyeenah	ham
говядина	gahvyahdyeenah	beef
жареная	zhahryeenahyah	roasted
отварная	ahtvahrnahyah	boiled
печёнка	pyeechyonkah	liver
почки	poch'kee	kidneys
ростбиф	rostbeef	roast beef
свинина	sveenyeenah	pork
свиные котлеты	sveeniyee kahtlyehti	pork chops
сосиски	sahsseeskee	sausage
телятина	tyeelyahtyeenah	veal

Game and fowl

I would like some game or fowl.	**Я бы взял дичи или птицы.**	yah bi vzyahl dyeechyee eelyee ptyeetsi
бекас	byehkahss	snipe
вальдшнеп	vahl'dshnehp	woodcock
гусь	goos'	goose
заяц	zahyahts	hare
индейка	eendyaykah	turkey
кролик	krolyeek	rabbit
курица	kooreetsah	chicken
куропатка	koorahpahtkah	partridge
перепел	pyehryeepyehl	quail
рябчик	ryahbchyeek	hazel-grouse
тетерев-косач	tyehtyeeryev	black grouse
утка	ootkah	duck
цыплёнок	tsiplyonahk	chicken

Russian meat dishes

бефстроганов, картофель «фри»	beefstrogahnahv kahrto-fyee' free	beef Stroganoff with chips (french fries)
бифштекс натуральный	beefshtehks nahtoorahl'niy	grilled beefsteak

EATING OUT

говядина тушёная с кореньями	gahvyahdyeenah toosho-nahyah s kahryehn'yahmee	beef braised with aromatic vegetables
голубцы	gahloobtsi	stuffed cabbage
гуляш	goolyahsh	goulash
жаркое из свинины со сливами	zharkoyeh eez svyeenyeeni sah slyeevahmee	roast pork with plums
котлеты натуральные из баранины	kahtlyehti nahtoorahl'niyeh eez bahrahnyeeni	grilled mutton chops
котлеты отбивные из баранины	kahtlyehti ahtbeevniyeh eez bahrahnyeeni	breaded mutton chops
котлеты свиные от-бивные	kahtlyehti sveeniyeh ahtbyeevniyeh	breaded pork chops
плов из баранины	plov eez bahrahnyeeni	rice with minced mutton
ростбиф с гарниром	rostbeef s gahrnyeerahm	roast beef with vegetables
шашлык	shashlik	shashlik, pieces of lamb grilled on skewers
шницель	shnyeetsehl'	breaded veal cutlet
язык	yeezik	tongue
язык отварной	yeezik ahtvahrnoy	boiled tongue of beef

How do you like your meat?

baked	жареное	zhahryeenahyeh
boiled	варёное	vahryonahyeh
braised	тушёное	tooshonahyeh
fried	жареное	zhahryeenahyeh
grilled	жареное на рашпере (вертеле)	zhahryeenahyeh nah rahshpyeeryeh (vyehrtyeelyeh)
roasted	жареное	zhahryeenahyeh
stewed	тушёное	tooshonahyeh
stuffed	фаршированное	fahrshirovahnahyeh

Game and fowl dishes

гусь с яблоками	goos' s **yahb**lahkahmee	goose with apples
индейка с яблоками	eend**yay**kah s **yahb**lah-kahmee	turkey with apples
котлеты из кур пожарские	kaht**lyeh**ti eez koor pah**zhahr**skeeyeh	minced chicken patties *Pozharsky* style
котлеты из куриного филе в сухарях	kaht**lyeh**ti eez koor**ee**nah-vah feel**yeh** v sookhah-**ryahk**	boned and breaded chicken breasts
котлеты по-киевски	kaht**lyeh**ti pah **kee**yehvskee	butter-stuffed chicken breasts
курица отварная с рисом	koo**ree**tsah ahtvahr**nah**yah s **ree**ssahm	boiled chicken with rice
куропатка жареная с вареньем	koorah**paht**kah **zhahr**yeenahyah s vahr**yehn'**yehm	roast partridge with jam
рябчики жареные с вареньем	**ryahb**chyeekee **zhahr**yee-niyeh s vahr**yehn'**yehm	broiled hazel-hen with jam
утка с тушёной капустой	**oot**kah s too**sho**nigh kah**poos**tigh	roast duck with stewed cabbage
утка с яблоками	**oot**kah s **yahb**lahkahmee	duck with apples
филе из кур фарши-рованное грибами	feel**yeh** eez koor fahrshiro-vahnahyeh gree**bah**mee	minced chicken patties with mushroom filling
филе куриное паровое с гребешками	feel**yeh** koor**ee**nahyeh pahrahvoyeh s gryeh-byehsh**kah**mee	boned chicken steamed with cock's combs
цыплёнок жареный с картофелем	tsi**plyo**nahk **zhahr**yeeniy s kahr**tof**yeelyehm	broiled chicken with potatoes
цыплята «табака»	tsi**plyah**tah tah**bah**kah	Georgian fried chicken
цыплята жареные в сметане	tsi**plyah**tah **zhahr**yeeniyeh v smyee**tah**nyeh	roast chicken in sour cream
чахохбили из кур	chyahkhokh**bee**lyeh eez koor	Caucasian casserole of chicken, served with tomatoes

Vegetables and seasonings

What vegetables do you recommend?	**Какие овощи вы советуете?**	kahkeeyeh ovahshchyee vi sahvyehtooeetyee
I'd prefer some salad.	**Я бы взял салат.**	yah bi vzyahl sahlaht

баклажаны	bahklahzhahni	aubergines (eggplant)
бобы	bahbi	broad beans
горох	gahrokh	peas
грибы	greebi	mushrooms
кабачки	kahbahch'kee	vegetable marrow (zucchini)
каперсы	kahpyehrsi	capers
картофель	kahrtofyehl'	potatoes
капуста	kahpoostah	cabbage
красная капуста	krahsnahyah kahpoostah	red cabbage
кукуруза	kookooroozah	maize (corn)
лук	look	onions
лук-порей	look pahryay	leeks
морковь	mahrkov'	carrots
овощи	ovahshchyee	vegetables
огурец	ahgooryehts	cucumber
перец	pyehreets	green pepper
перец горький	pyehreets gor'keey	pimentos
петрушка	pyeetrooshkah	parsley
помидоры	pahmeedori	tomatoes
редис	ryeedyeess	radishes
репа	ryehpah	turnips
рис	reess	rice
свёкла	svyoklah	beets
сельдерей	syeel'dyeeryay	celery
фасоль	fahssol'	french beans (green beans)
хрен	khryehn	horseradish
цветная капуста	tsvyehtnahyah kahpoostah	cauliflower
шпинат	shpeenaht	spinach

Fruit

Have you got fresh fruit?	У вас есть свежие фрукты?	oo vahss yehst' svyehzhiyeh **frook**ti
I'd like a fresh fruit salad.	Дайте мне, пожалуйста, фруктового салата.	**digh**tyee mnyeh pahzhah-loostah frook**to**vahvah sah**lah**tah

абрикосы	ahbree**kos**si	apricots
айва	**igh**vah	quince
ананас	ahnah**nahss**	pineapple
апельсины	ahpyeel'**see**ni	oranges
арбуз	ahr**booz**	watermelon
банан	bah**nahn**	banana
виноград	veenah**grahd**	grapes
вишни	**veesh**nyee	cherries
грейпфрут	**grayp**froot	grapefruit
грецкие орехи	**gryehts**keeyeh ahr**yehk**hee	walnuts
груша	**groo**shah	pear
дыня	**di**nyah	melon
клюква	**klyook**vah	cranberries
лимон	**lyee**mon	lemon
малина	mah**lyee**nah	raspberries
мандарины	mahndah**ree**ni	tangerines
маслины	mah**slyee**ni	olives
миндаль	meen**dahl'**	almonds
орехи	ahr**yehk**hee	hazelnuts
персики	**pyehr**seekee	peaches
сливы	**slyee**vi	plums
финики	**fee**nyeekee	dates

Dessert

If you've survived all the courses of the menu, you may want to say:

I'd like a dessert, please.	Пожалуйста, что-нибудь на третье.	pahzhah**loos**tah **shto**nyee-bood' nah **tryeht'**yeh
Something light, please.	Что-нибудь лёгкое, пожалуйста.	**shto**nyeebood' **lyokh**kah-yeh pahzhah**loos**tah
Nothing more, thanks.	Больше ничего, спасибо.	**bol'**shi nyeech**yeevo** spah**ssee**bah

If you aren't sure what to order, ask the waiter:

What do you recommend?	Что вы посоветуете?	shto vi pahssah**vyeh**too-eetyee

Russians, like the Americans and British, just love to top off their meal with something sweet. A typical dessert is кисель — **keessyehl'**. This is a compote made of cranberries, black currants, cherries or apples and thickened with potato starch. After cooking, the juices are strained and allowed to chill. The jelled juices are topped off with sugar, milk or cream. Ice-cream is another Soviet speciality.

блинчики с вареньем	blyeenchyeekee s vahryeh-n'yehm	pancakes filled with jam
компот	kahmpot	fruit compote
мороженое	mahrozhinahyeh	ice-cream
ванильное	vahnyeel'nahyeh	vanilla
фруктовое	frooktovahyeh	tutti-frutti
шоколадное	shikahlahdnahyeh	chocolate
оладьи с яблоками	ahlahd'yee s yahblahkahmee	apple puff
пирог с лимоном	peerog s lyeemonahm	lemon tart
ромовая баба	romahvahyah **bah**bah	cake steeped in rum and syrup
рисовый пудинг с киселём	**ree**ssahviy **poo**dyeeng s keessyeel**yom**	rice pudding with *kisel*
пирожные	peerozhniyeh	tea-cakes (cookies)
слоёный торт с фрук-товой начинкой	slah**yo**niy tort s frooktovigh nah**chyee**nkigh	shortcake
холодное какао	khahlodnahyeh kah**ka**ho	iced chocolate drink
холодное кофе	khah**lod**niy kofyeh	iced coffee
шоколадный бисквит	shikah**lahd**niy beess**kveet**	chocolate sponge cake
яблочный пирог	**yab**lahch'niy peer**og**	apple pie

The bill (check)

May I have the bill (check), please?	Пожалуйста, счёт.	pah**zhah**loostah shchyot
Haven't you made a mistake?	Вы не ошиблись?	vi nyee ah**shib**lyeess
Do you accept traveller's cheques?	Берёте ли вы дорож-ные чеки?	byee**ryo**tyee lyee vi dah**rozh**niyeh **chyeh**kee
Do you accept Intourist meal vouchers?	Берёте ли вы обе-денные талоны Интуриста?	bee**ryo**tyee lyee vi ah-**byeh**dyeenniyeh tah**lo**ni eentoo**ree**stah

How many meal vouchers must I give you?	Сколько вам дать обеденных талонов?	skol'kah vahm daht' ahbyehdyeennikh tahlonahv
I'll take my change in cigarettes (in chocolate).	Я хочу взять сдачу сигаретами (шоко-ладом).	yah khahchyoo vzyaht' zdahchyoo seegahryeh-tahmee (shikahlahdam)
That was a very good meal. We enjoyed it, thank you.	Было очень вкусно. Нам понравилось, спасибо.	bilah ochyeen' vkoosnah. nahm pahnrahvilahss spahsseebah

Complaints

But perhaps you'll have something to complain about…

Could you give us another table?	Дайте нам, пожа-луйста, другой столик.	dightyee nahm pahzhah-loostah droogoy stolyeek
That's not what I ordered. I asked for…	Я не это заказывал. Я заказал…	yah nyee ehtah zahkahzi-vahl. yah zahkahzal
I don't like this/ I can't eat this.	Мне это не нравится/ Я не могу этого есть.	mnyeh ehtah nyee nrah-veetsah/yah nyee mahgoo ehtahvah yest'
May I change this?	Дайте мне, пожа-луйста, что-нибудь другое.	dightyee mnyeh pahzhah-loostah shtonyeebood' droogoyeh
The meat is…	Мясо…	myahssah
overdone/under-done too rare/too tough	пережарено/недожа-рено сырое/жёсткое	pyeeryeezhahryeenah/ nyeedahzhahryeenah syroyeh/zhostkahyeh
This is too…	Это слишком…	ehtah slyeeshkahm
bitter/salty/sweet	горько/солоно/ сладко	gor'kah/solahnah/ slahdkah
The food is cold.	Еда холодная.	yeedah khahlodnahyah
This isn't fresh.	Это не свежее.	ehtah nyee svyehzhehyeh
Would you ask the head waiter to come over?	Позовите, пожа-луйста, мэтр д'отеля.	pahzahveetyee pahzhah-loostah mehtrdotehlyah

Drinks

Beer

Beer is especially popular in summertime among Russians when beer stalls are set up on the streets to quench the thirst of passersby. An inexpensive brand of Soviet beer found in smaller restaurants is *Zhigulevskoye*, but when dining out in elegant places you're likely to be offered one of these brands (all light beers):

рижское	**rizh**skahyeh	Rizhskoye
московское	mah**skov**skahyeh	Moskovskoye
ленинградское	lyehnyeen**grahd**skahyeh	Leningradskoye
двойное золотое	dvigh**noy**eh zah**lah**toyeh	Dvoinoye Zolotoye

If you want to order beer in a restaurant, you can either say "a bottle of beer" or "a beer". They only sell beer in half-litre (pint) bottles.

Bring me a bottle of beer, please.	**Принесите мне, пожалуйста, бутылку пива.**	preenyee**ssee**tyee mnyeh pah**zhah**loostah boo**til**koo **pee**vah
Light beer, please.	**Светлого пива, пожалуйста.**	**svyeht**lahvah **pee**vah pah**zhah**loostah
Do you have dark beer?	**Есть ли у вас тёмное пиво?**	yehst' lyee oo vahss **tyom**nahyeh **pee**vah

Vodka and cognac

Some Russians feel that a meal is incomplete without vodka—especially when appetizers are being served. A liquor made from wheat, vodka is colourless and looks like water. But watch out if you're invited to dinner by a Russian friend—you may find yourself under the table by the time you've had some *zakuskis* and a few glasses of vodka. This potent concoction is, in fact, meant to break the ice and get people to let their hair down—but a word to the wise is sufficient.

EATING OUT

Russians will gulp down several jiggers of vodka before entering into the main part of the meal. Unless you're a seasoned drinker, you'd better find some polite excuse for not accepting more than one glass.

It's traditional to propose toasts at Russian dinners. That's why we've given a few general suggestions on page 60. Of course, your Russian host will understand if you just raise your glass and smile.

Ordering hard liquor in the USSR is a bit different from the way it's done in the United States and in Great Britain. You just can't say: "Bring me a vodka, please." There's sure to be some misunderstanding unless you specify the exact quantity desired. The smallest portion of vodka or cognac you can order is 50 grams (equal to a single or a shot glass), the next graduation being 100 grams (like a double or double shot). On the other hand, you may order a glass of wine which usually equals 200 grams. A bottle of vodka or cognac normally contains about a pint, and a bottle of wine is generally about a pint and a half. With this in mind, you can say:

EATING OUT

I'd like 50 grams of vodka/cognac, please.	Дайте мне, пожалуйста, 50 граммов водки/коньяка.	**digh**tyee mnyeh pah**zhah**loostah 50 **grahm**mahv **vod**kee/kahnyee**kah**
I'd like 150 grams of the same, please.	Пожалуйста, 150 того-же самого.	pah**zhah**loostah 150 tah**vo** zheh **sah**mahvah
Bring me a bottle of…	Принесите мне, бутылку…	preenyee**ssee**tye mnyeh **boo**tilkoo
vodka	водки	**vod**kee
cognac	коньяку	kahnyee**koo**
wine	вина	vee**nah**

Note: Hard liquor is almost twice as expensive in restaurants as it is in stores. You can buy liquor over the counter from 11 a.m. onwards. The liquor counters in Soviet stores are often very, very crowded.

Don't expect to find exotic drinks in small cafés. For these you'll have to go to the more sophisticated bars and hotels. Here's what you may want to order:

aperitif	аперитив	ahpyehree**tyeev**
beer	пиво	**pee**vah
brandy	бренди	**breh**ndyee
cognac	коньяк	kah**nyahk**
gin	джин	dzhin
gin-fizz	джин-физ	**dzhin**-feez
gin and tonic	джин с тоником (тонизирующей водой)	dzhin s **to**nyeekahm (tah-nyee**zee**rooyooshchyay vah**doy**)
liqueur	ликёр	leek**yor**
port	портвейн	pahrt**vyayn**
rum	ром	rom
sherry	херес	**khyeh**ryehss
vermouth	вермут	**vyehr**moot
vodka	водка	**vod**kah
screwdriver	водка с апельсиновым соком	**vod**kah s ahpyeel'**seen**ahvim **so**kahm
whisky	виски	**vee**skee
neat (straight)/ on the rocks	натуральное/со льдом	nahtoo**rahl'**nahyeh/sah l'dom
whisky and soda	виски с содовой водой	**vee**skee s **so**dahvigh vah**doy**

glass	стакан	stah**kahn**
bottle	бутылка	boo**til**kah

But you should take this occasion to taste…

коньяк «Енисели»	kah**nyahk** yehnyee**ssyeh**lyee	brandy, of exceptional quality
коньяк «ОС»	kah**nyahk** o ehss	brandy, well aged
Мускат крымский	moos**kaht** **krim**skeey	Crimean red muscat wine
Салхино	**sahl**kheeno	red dessert wine
Чёрные глаза	**chyor**niyeh glah**zah**	"Dark Eyes"; red dessert wine
I'd like to try some Pertsovka,* please.	Я хотел бы попробовать перцовки.	yah khah**tyehl** bi pah**probi**vaht' pyeh**rtsov**kee

* a pepper-flavoured vodka

Are there any local specialities?	Есть ли что-нибудь местное или фирменное?	yehst' lyee **shto**nyeebood' **myehst**nahyeh **ee**lyee **feer**myeennahyeh

> **ЗА ВАШЕ ЗДОРОВЬЕ!**
> (zah **vah**sheh zdah**rov**'yeh)
>
> CHEERS!

EATING OUT

Here a few ideas for toasts when invited to a Russian dinner:

Here's to our host, Mr. ....!	За здоровье хозяина, господина...!	zah zdah**rov**'yeh khah**zyah**-eenah gahspah**dyee**nah
Here's to future co-operation between our organizations!	За наше будущее сотрудничество!	zah **nah**sheh boodoo-shchyeeyeeh sah**trood**-nyeechyeestvah
Health and happiness!	За ваше здоровье и благополучие!	zah **vah**sheh zdah**rov**'yeh ee blahgahpah**looch**'yeh

Wine

While vodka is still the Soviet Union's most popular drink, there is a growing trend toward wine-drinking. Vintners in the Crimean and Ukrainian regions are producing good imitations of champagne and port. Soviet-made champagne or sparkling wine has now become standard fare at all parties—even being served with ice-cream desserts. There's dry, slightly sweet and sweet sparkling wine, one of the best known of which is *Sovietskoye shampanskoye*.

One of the best white wines is *Tsinandali,* a dry wine from Georgia. That region also produces the well-known *Mukuzani,* a red table wine.

I'd like something...·	Я хотел-бы чего-нибудь...	yah khah**tyehl** bi chyeevo-nyeebood'
sweet/sparkling/dry	сладкого/шипучего/сухого	**slahd**kahvah/shi**poo**chyee-vah/**sookho**vah

I want a bottle of white wine.	Я хочу бутылку белого вина.	yah khah**chyoo** boo**til**koo **byeh**lahvah **vee**nah
I don't want anything too sweet.	Я не хочу ничего слишком сладкого.	yah nyee khah**chyoo** nyee-**chyee**vo **slyeesh**kahm **slahd**kahvah
How much is a bottle of…?	Сколько стоит бутылка…?	**skol**'kah **sto**eet boo**til**kah
That's too expensive.	Это слишком дорого.	**eh**tah **sleesh**kahm **do**rahgah
Haven't you anything cheaper?	Нет ли чего-нибудь подешевле?	nyeht lyee chyee**vo**nyee-bood' pahdyee**shehv**lyee
Fine, that'll do.	Хорошо. Это годится.	khahrah**sho**. **eh**tah gah-**dyee**tsah

If you enjoyed the wine, you may want to say:

Bring me another…, please.	Пожалуйста, ещё один (одну)…	pah**zhahl**oostah yee**shchyo** ah**dyeen** (ahd**noo**)
glass/carafe/bottle	стакан/графин/бутылку	stah**kahn**/grah**feen**/boo**til**koo
What's the name of this wine?	Как называется это вино?	kahk nahzi**vah**yeetsah **eh**tah **vee**no
Where does this wine come from?	Откуда это вино?	aht**koo**dah **eh**tah **vee**no
How old is this wine?	Какого года вино?	kah**ko**vah **go**dah **vee**no

dry	сухое	soo**kho**yeh
red	красное	**krahs**nahyeh
rosé	розовое	**ro**zahvahyeh
sparkling	шипучее	shi**poo**chyeeyeh
sweet	сладкое	**slahd**kahyeh
white	белое	**byeh**lahyeh
chilled	холодное	khah**lod**nahyeh
at room temperature	комнатной температуры	**kom**nahtnigh tyeeyempyee-**rah**toori

Tea

This beverage plays somewhat the same role in the USSR as it does in Great Britain. Certainly, the long Russian winter has a great deal to do with this. As soon as a Russian husband comes from work, his wife brings him a glass of hot tea. While the handsome samovar has now been replaced by a more ordinary teapot, a cup of hot tea on a wintry day helps thaw out both the people and the conversation.

Most Russians drink their tea in glasses. It's rather weak and served with lemon. Some put a spoonful of jam or honey in their tea.

Kvass

This is a non-alcoholic beverage that looks like dark beer and is made from black bread and yeast. Strangely enough, this drink is used as an ingredient in many Russian dishes. *Kvass* may or may not be sold in restaurants, as it's considered somewhat inelegant. But this typically Russian beverage can be sampled from little tank carts in the streets. There's usually a woman attendant seated beside the spigot, and you just get in line with the Russians. No language barrier here. All you need to say is:

| A small one, please. | Маленькую, пожа-луйста. | **mah**lyeen'kooyoo pah**zhah**-loostah |
| A big one, please. | Большую, пожалуй-ста. | bahl'**shoo**yoo pah**zhah**-loostah |

Other beverages

Nowadays there are many soft-drink dispensers on USSR street corners. The machines have one window for filling and one window for washing—everybody must use the same glass. The vending machines dispense carbonated fruit drinks, mineral water, beer, milk, coffee and cocoa.

If you want a delicious milk shake, visit a modern ice-cream parlour and ask for a фруктовый коктейль (frook**to**viy kahk-**tayl**').

I'd like a/some…	Дайте мне, пожалуй-ста…	**digh**tyee mnyeh pah**zhah**-loostah
cocoa	какао	kah**ka**ho
coffee	кофе	**ko**fyeh
cup of coffee	чашку кофе	**chyahsh**koo **ko**fyeh
with milk/without	с молоком/без	s mahlah**kom**/byehz
milk	молока	mahlah**kah**
Turkish coffee	кофе по-восточ-ному	**ko**fyeh pah vah**stoch**'-nahmoo
cranberry juice	клюквенный морс	**klyook**vyeeniy mors
fruit juice	фруктовый сок	frook**to**viy sok
apple	яблочный	**yahb**lahshniy
cherry	вишневый	veesh**nyo**viy
grape	виноградный	veenah**grahd**niy
grapefruit	грейпфрутовый	**grayp**frootahviy
orange	апельсиновый	apyeel'**syee**nahviy
pomegranate	гранатовый	grah**nah**tahviy
prune	сливовый	**slyee**voviy
tangerine	мандариновый	mahnda**ree**nahviy
kvass	квасу	**kvah**ssoo
lemonade	лимонада	lyeemah**nah**dah
milk	молока	mahlah**kah**
milk shake	фруктовый коктейль	frook**to**viy kahk**tayl**'
sour milk	кефира	kyee**fee**rah
mineral water	минеральной воды	meenyeer**ahl**'nigh vah**di**
tea	чай	**chyigh**
with lemon	с лимоном	s lee**mo**nahm
with milk	с молоком	s mahlah**kom**
with honey	с мёдом	s **myo**dahm
with jam	с вареньем	s vah**ryehn**'yehm

Eating light—Snacks

You may not feel like having a big meal in a restaurant and may just want a quick bite in a буфет (boo**fyeht**—snack bar) or пирожковая (peerahzh**ko**vahyah—eating-place serving turnovers with savoury fillings). Since most of the snacks are on display, you won't need to say much more than:

I'll have one of those, please.	Дайте мне один такой пожалуйста.	**dight**yee mnyeh ah**dyeen** tah**koy** pah**zhah**loostah
Give me two of those and one of those.	Дайте мне, пожалуйста, два таких и один такой.	**dight**yee mnyeh pah**zhah**loostah dvah tahk**yeekh** ee ah**dyeen** takoy
to the left/to the right above/below	слева/справа наверху/внизу	**slyeh**vah/**sprah**vah nahvyeer**khoo**/vnyee**zoo**
Give me a/an/ some…, please.	Дайте мне, пожалуйста…	**dight**yee mnyeh pah**zhah**loostah
biscuits (cookies)	печенья	pyee**chyehn**′yah
bread	хлеба	**khlyeh**bah
black bread	черного хлеба	**chyor**nahvah **khlyeh**bah
whole-wheat bread	белого хлеба	**byeh**lahvah **khlyeh**bah
butter	масла	**mahs**lah
chocolate (bar)	шоколада (плитку)	shikah**lah**dah (**plyeet**koo)
Dutch-style cheese	сыр	sir
eggs	яйца	**yight**sah
frankfurters	сосисок	sahs**see**ssahk
Russian type frankfurter	сардельки	sahr**dyel**′kee
ice-cream	мороженого	mah**ro**zhinahvah
kasha (porridge)	каши	**kah**shi
meat pie	паштета	pahsh**tyeh**tah
pastry	пирожное	peero**zhn**ahyeh
pie	пирога	peerah**gah**
plum cake	кекс	kyehks
roll	булочку	**boo**lahch′koo
sandwich	бутерброд	booteer**brod**
cheese sandwich	бутерброд с сыром	booteer**brod** s **si**rahm
ham sandwich	бутерброд с ветчиной	booteer**brod** s vee-**chyee**noy
caviar sandwich	бутерброд с икрой	booteer**brod** s eek**roy**
sweet cream cheese	сырок	**si**rok
turnover	пирожок	peerah**zhok**
How much is that?	Сколько это стоит?	**skol**′kah **eh**tah **sto**eet

EATING OUT

Travelling around

Plane

While the stewardesses on Aeroflot planes aren't as willowy as their western counterparts, they're just as friendly and helpful. The only trouble is that some of the Russian girls don't speak English fluently. Here are a few useful expressions:

Do you speak English?	Вы говорите по-английски?	vi gahvah**reet**yee pah ahng**lyeey**skee
Is there a flight to Leningrad?	Есть ли рейс на Ленинград?	yehst′ lyee ryayss nah lyehnyeen**grahd**
When's the next plane to Kiev?	Когда отлетает следующий самолёт в Киев?	kahg**dah** ahtlyee**tah**yeht **slyeh**dooshchyeey sahmah**lyot** v **kee**yehv
I'd like a ticket to Moscow.	Дайте мне, пожа-луйста, билет до Москвы.	**dight**yee mnyeh pah**zhah**-loostah bee**lyeht** dah mah**skvi**
What's the fare to Baku?	Сколько стоит билет до Баку?	**skol′**kah **stoy**eet bee**lyeht** dah bah**koo**
single (one-way) return (round trip)	в один конец туда и обратно	v ah**dyeen** kah**nyehts** too**dah** ee ah**braht**nah
What time does the plane take off?	В котором часу отле-тает самолёт?	v kah**tor**ahm chyee**ssoo** aht-lyee**tah**yeht sahmah**lyot**
What time do I have to check in?	В котором часу я должен зарегистри-ровать багаж?	v kah**tor**ahm chyee**ssoo** yah **dol**zhin zahryeegee**stree**-rahvaht′ bah**gahzh**
What's the flight number?	Какой номер рейса?	kah**koy no**myeer **ryay**ssah
I'd like some more coffee/a cognac.	Дайте мне, пожа-луйста ещё кофе/коньяку.	**dight**yee mnyeh pah**zhah**-loostah yee**shchyo ko**fyeh/kahnye**ekoo**

And on the plane ...

I feel sick.	Я себя плохо чув-ствую.	yah syee**byah plo**khah **chyoost**vooyoo
Where's the toilet?	Где туалет?	gdyeh tooah**lyeht**

Train

The Soviet Union is a huge country and anyone planning to travel by train had better be prepared to keep up a brave face hour after hour. While far more interesting and enlightening, train travel imposes a greater strain on your linguistic ability and your resourcefulness. Generally, your ticket reservations will be made in advance, and the Intourist Service Bureau in your hotel can handle any of your travel requests. You may want to take short train rides from the city where you're staying out to the suburbs. For this, be sure to check with your Intourist representative on travel limits to be observed. You'll find Russia's train stations animated and exciting places where you can glimpse the diversity of the Soviet people. For the serious observer, the train station is a fine place to study Russian ways and traditions.

Types of trains

Экспресс (ehks**prehss**)	Long-distance express with luxury coaches; stops only at main stations; fare is higher
Скорый поезд (**sko**riy poeezd)	Standard long-distance train, stopping at main stations; fare is higher
Пассажирский поезд (pahssah**zh**irskeey poeezd)	Inter-city train; doesn't stop at very small stations; regular fare. This type of train is seldom available for tourist travel
Электричка (ehlyeek**treech**'kah)	Local train stopping at almost every station
Международный вагон (myehzhdoonah**rod**niy vah**gon**)	Sleeper with individual compartments (usually double) and washing facilities
Мягкий вагон (**myahkh**kyeey vah**gon**)	Sleeper with individual compartments (for two or four persons)
Купейный вагон (koo**pyay**niy vah**gon**)	Car with compartments for four persons; berths with blankets and pillows
Вагон-ресторан (vah**gon** ryeestah**rahn**)	Dining-car

To the railway station

Where's the railway station?	Где вокзал?	gdyeh vahg**zahl**
Taxi, please!	Такси!	tah**see**
Take me to the railway station.	К вокзалу, пожалуйста.	k vahg**zah**loo pah**zhah**loo-stah

Tickets

In reality, there's no first or second class on Soviet trains. However, the railway does offer a type of accommodation which is better than the standard and roughly corresponds to first class on the Continent.

Where's the...?	Где...?	gdyeh
information office	справочное бюро	**sprah**vahch'nahyeh byooro
reservations office	бюро предварительной продажи билетов	byoo**ro** pryeedvah**ree**tyehl'-noy prah**dah**zhi bee**lyeh**-tahv
ticket office	билетная касса	bee**lyeht**nahyah **kahs**sah
I want a ticket to Rostov, second-class return (round trip).	Дайте мне, пожалуйста, билет до Ростова, купейный, туда и обратно.	**digh**tyee mnyeh pah**zhah**-loostah bee**lyeht** dah rah-**sto**vah koo**pyay**niy too**dah** ee ah**braht**nah
I'd like two singles (one-way) to Volgograd.	Мне нужно два билета в один конец до Волгограда.	mnyeh **noozh**nah dvah bee**lyeh**tah v ah**dyeen** kah-**nyehts** dah volgah**grah**dah
How much is the fare to Odessa?	Сколько стоит билет до Одессы?	**skol**'kah **sto**eet bee**lyeht** dah ah**dyehs**si

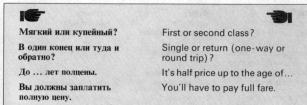

Мягкий или купейный?	First or second class?
В один конец или туда и обратно?	Single or return (one-way or round trip)?
До ... лет полцены.	It's half price up to the age of...
Вы должны заплатить полную цену.	You'll have to pay full fare.

TRAVELLING AROUND

Further inquiries

Is it a through train?	Это прямой поезд?	ehtah pryeemoy poeezd
Does this train stop at Minsk?	Останавливается ли этот поезд в Минске?	ahstahnahvlyeevahyehtsah lyee ehtaht poeezd v meenskyeh
When is the ... train to Volgograd?	Когда... поезд на Волгоград?	kahgdah ... poeezd nah volgahgrahd
first/last/next	первый/последний/следующий	pyehrviy/pahslyehdnyeey/slyehdooshchyeey
What time does the train from Riga arrive?	В котором часу приходит поезд из Риги?	v kahtorahm chyeessoo preekhodyeet poeezd eez reeghee
What time does the train for Gorki leave?	В котором часу отходит поезд на Горький?	v kahtorahm chyeessoo ahtkhodyeet poeezd nah gor'keey
Will the train leave on time?	Поезд отойдёт по расписанию?	poeezd ahtighdyot pah rahspeessahn'yoo
Is there a dining-car on the train?	Есть ли в этом поезде вагон-ресторан?	yehst' lyee v ehtahm poeezdyeh vahgon-ryeestahrahn

ВХОД	ENTRANCE
ВЫХОД	EXIT
К ПЕРРОНАМ	TO THE PLATFORMS

Where's the...

Where's the...?	Где...?	gdyeh
buffet	буфет	boofyeht
restaurant	ресторан	ryeestahrahn
left luggage office (baggage check)	камера хранения	kahmyeerah khrahnyeh-n'yah
lost property office (lost and found)	бюро находок	byooro nahkhodahk
news-stand	газетный киоск	gahzyehtniy keeosk
waiting room	зал ожидания	zahl ahzhidahn'yah
Where are the toilets?	Где туалет?	gdyeh tooahlyeht

Platform

What platform does the train for Leningrad leave from?	С какой платформы отходит поезд на Ленинград?	s kahkoy plahtformi ahtkhodyeet poeezd nah lyehnyeengrahd
What platform does the train from Odessa arrive at?	На какую платформу приходит поезд из Одессы?	nah kahkooyoo plahtfor-moo preekhodyeet poeezd eez ahdyehssi
Where's platform 7?	Где платформа номер 7?	gdyeh plahtformah nomyeer 7
Is this the right platform for the train to...?	Поезд на... отходит с этой платформы?	poeezd nah ... ahtkhodyeet s ehtigh plahtformi

Это прямой поезд.	It's a direct train.
Пересадка в...	You have to change at...
В ... вы должны пересесть на местный поезд.	Change at ... and get a local train.
Платформа номер...	Platform... is...
там/внизу слева/справа	over there/downstairs on the left/on the right
Поезд на ... отходит в ... с платформы номер...	The train to ... will leave at ... from platform...
Поезд №... на Брест опаздывает на ... минут.	The ... train for Brest will be ... minutes late.
Поезд опаздывает на ... минут.	There'll be a delay of ... minutes.

TRAVELLING AROUND

FOR NUMBERS, see page 175

All aboard

Excuse me. May I get past?	**Разрешите пройти.**	rahzree**shi**tyee prigh**tyee**
Is this seat taken?	**Это место занято?**	**eh**tah **myeh**stah **zah**nyahtah
Is this seat free?	**Это место свободно?**	**eh**tah **myeh**stah svah**bod**nah

---

НЕ КУРИТЬ
NO SMOKING

I think that's my seat.	**По-моему, это моё место.**	pah **moy**moo **eh**tah ma**hyo myeh**stah
Can you tell me when we get to Odessa?	**Скажите мне, пожалуйста, когда мы прибудем в Одессу?**	skah**zhi**tyee mnyeh pah**zhah**loostah kahg**dah** mi pree**boo**dyeem v ah**dyehs**-soo
What station is this?	**Какая это станция?**	kah**kah**yah **eh**tah **stahn**-tsiyah
How long does the train stop here?	**Сколько здесь стоит поезд?**	**skol**'kah zdyehs' stah**eet po**eezd
When do we get to Rostov?	**Когда мы прибудем в Ростов?**	kahg**dah** mi pree**boo**dyeem v rah**stov**

Some time on the journey the ticket-collector (контролер— kahntrah**lyor**) will come around and say:

| Tickets, please! | **Ваши билеты, пожалуйста!** | **vah**shi beel**yeh**ti pah**zhah**loostah |

Eating

There's usually a dining car on long-distance trains where you can get meals and drinks. The проводник (prahvahd**nyeek**— steward) will serve you tea at standard prices. On many trains an attendant comes around with snacks, biscuits (cookies) and soft drinks.

| Where's the dining car, please? | Где вагон-ресторан? | gdyeh vah**gon**-ryeestah-**rahn** |
| Will you give me a cup of tea, please? | Дайте мне, пожалуйста, стакан чаю. | **dight**yee mnyeh pah**zhah**-loostah stah**kahn chyah**yoo |

Sleeping

Your berth will have to be booked in advance. It's customary for the steward to bring you a cup of tea in the morning. If you want coffee, you ought to bring along some instant coffee.

Are there any free compartments in the sleeping car?	Есть ли свободное купе в спальном вагоне?	yehst' lyee svah**bod**nahyeh koo**peh** v **spahl'**nahm vah**gon**yeh
Where's the sleeping car?	Где спальный вагон?	gdyeh **spahl'**niy vah**gon**
Where's my berth?	Где моя полка?	gdyeh mah**yah pol**kah
Can you give me another berth?	Нет ли другой полки?	nyet lyee droo**goy pol**kyee
I'd like a lower berth.	Я хотел бы нижнюю полку.	yah khah**tyehl** bi **nyeezh**-nyooyoo **pol**koo
Would you make up our berths?	Постелите нам, пожалуйста.	pahstyee**lyee**tyee nahm pah**zhah**loostah
Would you call me at 7 o'clock?	Разбудите меня, пожалуйста, в семь часов утра.	rahzboo**dyee**tyee myee**nyah** pah**zhah**loostah v syehm' chyee**ssov oo**trah
Would you bring me some tea in the morning?	Могли бы вы мне принести утром чай?	mahg**lyee** bi vi mnyeh preenyee**stee oo**trahm chyigh

Baggage and porters

| Can you help me with my bags? | Возьмите, пожалуйста, мои чемоданы. | vahz'**myee**tyee pah**zhah**-loostah mah**ee** chyeemah-**dah**ni |
| Put them down here, please. | Поставьте их сюда, пожалуйста. | pah**stahv**tyee eekh syoo**dah** pah**zhah**loostah |

FOR PORTERS, also see page 24

Lost!

We hope you'll have no need for the following phrases on your trip... but just in case:

Where's the lost property office (lost and found)?	**Где бюро находок?**	gdyeh byoo**ro** nah**kho**dahk
I've lost my...	**Я потерял ...**	yah pahtyee**ryahl**
this morning yesterday	**сегодня утром вчера**	see**vod**nyah oo**trahm** vchyee**rah**
It's very valuable.	**Эта вещь очень ценная.**	**eh**tah vyehshch' **o**chyeen' **tsehn**nahyah

Time-tables

If you intend to do a lot of train travel, it might be a good idea to buy a time-table. These are based on the 24-hour clock and are for sale at ticket offices, information desks and in some bookshops.

I'd like to buy a time-table.	**Я хотел бы купить расписание.**	yah khah**tyehl** bi koo**peet'** rahspee**ssahn**'yeh

Underground (subway)

Unlike the subways of the U.S.A. or the underground of London, the Moscow метро (my**ee**tro) is beautifully decorated, clean and quiet. Its enormous escalators take you on a trip seemingly to the centre of the earth. The fare is the same, regardless of the distance or the numbers of transfers made.

Where's the nearest underground (subway) station?	**Где ближайшее метро?**	gdyeh blyee**zhigh**shcheh-yeh my**ee**tro
Does this train go to...?	**Этот поезд идёт до...?**	**eh**taht **po**eezd ee**dyot** dah
Where do I change for...?	**Где мне сделать пересадку на...?**	gdyeh mnyeh **sdyeh**laht' pyehryee**ssahd**koo nah
Is the next station...?	**Следующая станция...?**	**slyeh**dooshchyahyah **stahn**tsiyah

TRAVELLING AROUND

Bus—Tramway (Streetcar)

You'll find a ticket-dispensing machine on most buses. People are apparently very honest about paying and when the bus is crowded you'll be asked to pass 5-kopeck pieces towards the machine. Unlike bus drivers in most countries, Russian bus drivers wear no uniform.

Where can I get the bus to Kalinina Avenue?	Где мне сесть на автобус до проспекта Калинина?	gdyeh mnyeh syehs't' nah ahvtobooss dah prahspyehktah kahlyeenyeenah
What bus do I take for the ... Hotel?	На каком автобусе я могу доехать до гостиницы...?	nah kahkom ahvtoboossyeh yah mahgoo dahyehkhaht' dah gahstyeenyeetsi
Where's the...?	Где...?	gdyeh
bus stop terminus	остановка автобуса конечная остановка	ahstahnovkah ahvtoboossa kahnyehch'nahyah ahstahnovkah
When's the ... bus to Moscow State University?	Когда идёт... автобус к Московскому университету?	kahgdah eedyot ahvtobooss k mahskovskahmoo oonyeevyehrseetyehtoo
first/last/next	первый/последний/следующий	pyehrviy/pahslyehdneey/slyehdooshchyeey
How often do the buses to Lenin Library run?	Как часто идут автобусы к Ленинской библиотеке?	kahkchyahstaheedootahvtoboossi k lyehnyeenskigh beeblyeeahtyehkyeh
Do I have to change buses?	Нужно мне делать пересадку?	noozhnah mnyeh dyelaht' pyehryeessahdkoo
How long does the journey take?	Сколько мне ехать?	skol'kah mnyeh yehkhaht'
Please pass this coin to the machine.	Пожалуйста, передайте деньги на билет.	pahzhahloostah pyeeryeedightyee dyehn'ghee nah byeelyeht
Can you give me change for the ticket machine?	Не разменяете ли вы мне деньги на билет?	nyee rahzmyeenyahеetyee lyee vi mnyeh dyen'ghee nah beelyeht
Will you tell me when to get off?	Вы мне скажете, когда сходить?	vi mneh skahzhityee kahgdah skhahdyeet'

I want to get off at the Kremlin.	Я хочу сойти у Кремля.	yah khah**chyoo sigh**tyee oo kryehml**yah**
Are you getting off at the next stop?	Вы сходите на следующей?	vi s**kho**dyeetyee nah **sleh**dooshchyay
May I have my luggage, please?	Подайте мне, пожалуйста, мой чемодан.	pah**dight**yee mnyeh pah**zhah**loostah moy chyeemah**dahn**

ОСТАНОВКА	BUS STOP
ОСТАНОВКА ПО ТРЕБОВАНИЮ	STOPS ON REQUEST

Riverboats—Cruise ships

You can arrange to see the Soviet Union by boat. This way you get to know Russian ways even before landing in the country. Once in the USSR, you can take a long cruise down the Volga River. The riverboats feature solariums, swimming pools, evening dances on deck. Try a hydrofoil boat on the Moscow River.

When does the boat sail?	Когда отходит пароход?	kahg**dah** aht**kho**dyeet pahrah**khod**
I'd like to go ashore.	Я хотел бы сойти на берег.	yah khah**tyehl** bi **sigh**tyee nah **byeh**ryehg
Where's my cabin?	Где моя каюта?	gdyeh mah**yah** kah**yoo**tah
Does the boat stop at Volgograd?	Пароход останавливается в Волгограде?	pahrah**khod** ahstahn**ahv**-lyeevaheetsah v volgah-**grah**dyeh
What town is this?	Какой это город?	kah**koy eh**tah **go**rahd
We'd like to rent a car for the day.	Мы хотим взять машину напрокат на сегодняшний день.	mi khah**tyeem** vzyaht' mah**shi**noo nahprah**kaht** nah see**vod**nyeeshnyeey dyehn'

TRAVELLING AROUND

Around and about—Sightseeing

Your prepaid Intourist travel arrangements entitle you to one or more guided tours. For such excursions you should consult the Intourist Service Bureau at your hotel.

Here we're more concerned with the cultural aspect of life than with entertainment, and, for the moment, with towns rather than the countryside. If you want a guide-book, ask…

Can you recommend a good guide book for…?	Могли бы вы мне указать хороший путеводитель по…?	mahg**lyee** bi vi mnyeh ookah**zaht'** khah**ro**shiy pootyeevah**dyee**tyehl' pah
Is there an Intourist office?	Есть ли здесь бюро Интуриста?	yest' lyee zdyehs' byoo**ro** eentoo**ree**stah
What are the main points of interest?	Какие здесь главные достопримечатель-ности?	kah**kee**yeh zdyehs' **glahv**niyeh dahstahpree-myee**chyah**tyeel'nahstyee
We're only here for…	Мы здесь только на…	mi zdyehs' **tol**'kah nah
a few hours a day a week	несколько часов день неделю	**nyeh**skahl'kah chyee**ssov** dyehn' nyeed**yeh**lyoo
Can you recommend a sightseeing tour?	Как вы думаете, стоит осматривать достопримеча-тельности?	kahk vi **doo**mahyehtyeh **sto**eet ahsmahtreevaht' dahstahpreemyee**chyah**-tyeelnahstyee
Where does the bus start from?	Откуда отходит автобус?	ahtkoodah ahtkhodyeet ahvtobooss
Will it pick us up at the hotel?	Заедут ли за нами в гостиницу?	zah**yeh**doot lyee zah **nah**myee v gahs**tyee**nyeetsoo
What bus/tram (streetcar) should we get?	Какой нам нужен автобус/трамвай?	kah**koy** nahm **noo**zhin ahvtobooss/trahm**vigh**
How much does the tour cost?	Сколько это стоит?	skol'kah ehtah **sto**eet
What time does the tour start?	Когда начинается экскурсия?	kahg**dah** nahchyee**nahee**-tsah ehks**koor**seeyah

FOR TIME OF DAY, see page 178

Is there an English-speaking guide?	**Есть ли гид, говорящий по-английски?**	yehst' lyee gheed gahvah-**ryah**shchyeey pah ahn-**glyey**skee
Where is/Where are the...?	**Где находится/Где находятся...?**	gdyeh nah**kho**dyeetsah/ gdyeh nah**kho**dyahtsah
art gallery	**картинная галерея**	kah**rteen**nahyah gahlyee-**ryeh**yah
Bolshoi Theatre	**Большой Театр**	bahl'**shoy** tyee**ahtr**
castle	**замок**	**zah**mahk
cemetery	**кладбище**	**klahd**beeshchyeh
church	**церковь**	**tsehr**kahf'
city centre	**центр города**	tsehntr **go**rahdah
concert hall	**концертный зал**	kahn**tsehrt**niy zahl
convent	**монастырь**	mahnah**stir'**
docks	**пристань**	**pree**stahn
exhibition	**выставка**	**vi**stahvkah
factory	**фабрика**	**fahb**reekah
fortress	**крепость**	**kryeh**pahst'
fountain	**фонтан**	fahn**tahn**
gardens	**сады**	sah**di**
GUM department store	**Гум**	goom
harbour	**порт**	port
Kremlin	**Кремль**	**kryehml'**
lake	**озеро**	**o**zyeerah
law courts	**суд**	sood
Lenin Library	**Ленинская библиотека**	**lyehn**yeenskahyah beeblyee**ahtyeh**kah
market	**рынок**	**ri**nahk
memorial	**памятник**	**pah**myeetnyeek
Metro station	**станция метро**	**stahnt**siyah myee**tro**
monastery	**монастырь**	mahnah**stir'**
monument	**монумент**	mahnoo**myehnt**
Mosfilm studios	**киностудия Мосфильм**	keenah**stood**yeeyah mos**feel'**m
Museum of the Revolution	**Музей Революции**	moozyay reevah**lyoo**-tsiee
observatory	**обсерватория**	ahbsyehrvah**tor**eeyah
opera house	**оперный театр**	**o**pyehrniy tyee**ahtr**
palace	**дворец**	dvah**ryehts**
park	**парк**	pahrk
planetarium	**планетарий**	plahnyee**tah**reey
post-office	**почта**	**poch'**tah
Red Square	**Красная Площадь**	**krahs**nahyah **plo**shchyahd'
ruins	**развалины**	rah**zvah**lyeeni

stadium	стадион	stahdyee**on**
statue	статуя	**stah**tooyah
temple	храм	khrahm
theatre	театр	tyee**ah**tr
tomb	могила	mahg**hee**lah
tower	башня	**bah**shnyah
town centre	центр города	tsehntr **go**rahdah
town hall	горсовет	gorsah**vyeht**
university	университет	oonyeevyehrsee**tyeht**
vineyards	виноградники	veenah**grahd**nyeekee
zoo	зоопарк	zahah**pahrk**

Admission

Is the ... open on Sundays?	Открыт ли... по воскресеньям?	ahtkrit lyee ... pah vahskrees**syehn'**yahm
When does it open?	Когда открывается?	kahg**dah** ahtkrivah**eet**sah
When does it close?	Когда закрывается?	kahg**dah** zahkrivah**eet**sah
How much is the admission charge?	Сколько стоит билет?	**skol'**kah **sto**eet beel**yeht**
Is there any reduction for...?	Есть ли скидка для...?	yehst' lyee **skeed**kah dlyah
students/children	студентов/детей	stood**yehn**tahv/dyeet**yay**
Have you a guide book (in English)?	Есть ли у вас путеводитель (по-английски)?	yehst' lyee oo vahss pootyeevah**dyee**tyehl' (pahahn**glyeey**skee)
Can I buy a catalogue?	Я хочу купить каталог.	yah khakh**chyoo** koo**peet'** kahtah**log**
Is it all right to take pictures?	Можно ли снимать?	**mozh**nah lyee snyee**maht'**

| ВХОД БЕСПЛАТНЫЙ/ СВОБОДНЫЙ | ADMISSION FREE |
| ФОТОГРАФИРОВАТЬ ВОСПРЕЩАЕТСЯ | NO CAMERAS ALLOWED |

Who—What—When?

What's that building?	Что это за здание?	shto **ehtah** zah **zdahn'**yeh
Who was the...?	Кто был...?	kto bil
architect	архитектор	ahrkhee**teyhkt**ahr
painter	художник	khoo**dozh**nyeek
sculptor	скульптор	**skool'p**tahr
Who painted that picture?	Кто написал эту картину?	kto nahpee**ssahl ehtoo** kahr**tyee**noo
When did he live?	Когда он жил?	kahg**dah** on zhil
When was it built?	Когда это было построено?	kahg**dah ehtah** bilah pahs**troee**nah
Where's the house where ... lived?	Где дом, в котором жил...?	gdyeh dom v kah**tor**ahm zhil
We're interested in ...	Мы интересуемся...	mi eentyeeryee**ssoo-eem**syah
antiques	старинным бытом	stah**reen**nim bitahm
archaeology	археологией	ahrkheeah**log**heeyay
art	искусством	ees**koost**vahm
ballet	балетом	bah**lyeh**tahm
ceramics	керамикой	kyee**rah**meekigh
coins	нумизматикой	noomyeez**mah**tyeekigh
fine arts	изобразительным искусством	eezahbrah**zee**tyeel'nim ees**koost**vahm
furniture	мебелью	**myeh**byehl'yoo
geology	геологией	gheeah**log**heeyay
history	историей	ees**tor**eeyay
icons	иконами	ee**kon**ahmee
medicine	медициной	myehd**yeet**sinigh
music	музыкой	**moo**zikigh
natural history	естествознанием	yehs**tyeh**stvah**znah**nyee-yehm
ornithology	орнитологией	ahrnyeetah**log**heeyay
painting	живописью	**zhi**vapyeess'yoo
pottery	керамикой	kyee**rah**meekigh
sculpture	скульптурой	skool'p**too**righ
wild life	природой	pree**rod**igh
zoology	зоологией	zo-o**log**heeyay
Where's the ... department?	Где отдел...?	gdyeh aht**dyehl**

SIGHTSEEING

Just the adjective you've been looking for ...

It's ...	Это...	ehtah
amazing	**поразительно**	pahrah**zeet**yeel'nah
awful	**ужасно**	oo**zhahs**nah
beautiful	**прекрасно**	pryee**krahs**nah
hideous	**отвратительно**	ahtvrah**teet**yeel'nah
interesting	**интересно**	eentyee**ryehs**nah
magnificent	**великолепно**	vyeelyeekah**lyehp**nah
overwhelming	**непреодолимо**	nyeepreeahdah**lyee**mah
sinister	**скверно**	**skvyehr**nah
strange	**удивительно**	oodyee**veet**yeel'nah
stupendous	**изумительно**	eezoo**meet**yeel'nah
superb	**великолепно**	vyeelyeekah**leyhp**nah
terrible	**страшно**	**strahsh**nah
ugly	**безобразно**	byeezah**brahz**nah

Church services

Most churches are open to the public. The worshippers in Orthodox churches—by far the most prevalent—are generally old women. Whether by design or by accident, Moscow's modern skyscrapers are often found next to some little Orthodox church with its quaint whitewashed walls and gilded cupolas. When entering a church, women must wear a scarf on their heads. As there are no chairs or pews, the longer services are hard on the legs.

Is there a/an ... near here?	**Есть ли тут поблизости...?**	yehst' lyee toot pah**blyee**zahstyee
Baptist church	**баптистский молитвенный дом**	bahp**tyees**skeey mah**lyeet**vyeenniy dom
Catholic church	**католическая церковь**	kahtah**leech**yeeskahyah **tsehr**kahf'
Orthodox church	**православная церковь**	prahvah**slahv**nahyah **tsehr**kahf'
synagogue	**синагога**	seenah**gog**ah
Can I visit the church?	**Можно ли пойти в церковь?**	**mozh**nah lyee pigh**tyee** v **tsehr**kahf'
Where can I find a clergyman who speaks English?	**Где найти священника, который говорит по-английски?**	gdyeh nigh**tyee** svyee**shchyehn**nyeeka kah**tor**iy gahvah**reet** pah ahn**glyee**yeeskee

Relaxing

Cinema (movies)

The first showing at most cinemas starts at 9 a.m. and the last film may finish at midnight. There's a brief intermission after the newsreel, just before the main film starts. You may find a snack bar in the lobby.

A film schedule can be found in the newspaper Вечерняя Москва (vyee**chyehr**nyeeyah mahs**kvah**—Moscow's evening newspaper) or the English-language weekly, *Moscow News*.

Should you lose your way en route to the cinema, ask directions at a справочное бюро (**sprah**vahch'nahyeh byoo**ro**—information office) which are glass-enclosed stands located near main intersections. The woman inside has telephone books, maps and street guides at her disposal. She'll write directions on a scrap of paper in exchange for a few kopecks. If you have a map and can read Cyrillic characters, these information booths will help you get around.

Give me a copy of Vyechernaya Moskva, please.	Дайте мне, пожалуй-ста, «Вечернюю Москву».	**digh**tyee mnyeh pah**zhah**loostah vyee**chyehr**nyoo-yoo mahs**kvoo**
What's playing at the Mir Cinema tonight?	Что идёт сегодня вечером в кино «Мир»?	shto eed**yot** seevo**dnya**h **vyeh**chyeerahm v kee**no** meer
What sort of film is it?	Что это за фильм?	shto **eh**tah zah feel'm
Can you recommend a …?	Не могли бы вы посоветовать…?	nyee mahg**lyee** bi vi pahssah**vyeh**tahvaht'
good film	хороший фильм	khah**ro**shiy feel'm
comedy	комедию	kah**myeh**dyeeyoo
musical	музыкальное ревю	moozi**kahl'**nahyeh ryeh**vyoo**
drama	драму	**drah**moo
documentary	документальный фильм	dahkoomyehn**tahl'**niy feel'm

RELAXING

Theatre

Theatregoing is something worth doing even if you don't know Russian very well. You might try seeing a play you've already seen in English—let's say, one of Chekhov's or Shakespeare's works. The most well-known theatres are the Maly Theatre and the Moscow Art Theatre (MXAT). For avant-garde plays, there are the Theatre on Taganka and the Sovremennik Theatre. If you're travelling with your family, don't miss going to the Kukolny (puppet) Theatre and the Central Children's Theatre.

The Moscow theatre schedule appears in *Pravda*. There are matinées and evening performances—usually beginning at 7 p.m. sharp. Certain plays may be sold out for weeks in advance. There are two or three intermissions and you can go to the buffet for snacks.

Where is that Chekhov play being given?	Где идёт эта пьеса Чехова?	gdyeh eedyot ehtah p'yehssah chyehkhahvah
Who's playing the lead?	Кто играет главную роль?	kto eegraheet glahvnooyoo rol'
Who's the director?	Кто режиссёр?	kto ryehzhissyor
What time does it begin?	Когда начало?	kahgdah nahchyahlah
Are there any tickets for tonight?	Есть ли ещё билеты на сегодня?	yhest' lyee yeeshchyo beelyehti nah seevodnyah
I want a seat in the stalls (orchestra).	Я хочу место в первых рядах.	yah khahchyoo myehstah v pyehrvikh ryeedahkh
Not too far back.	Не слишком далеко от сцены.	nyee slyeeshkahm dahlyeeko aht stsehni
On the aisle.	У прохода.	oo prahkhodah
Somewhere in the middle.	Где-нибудь посредине.	gdyehnyeebood' pahsryeedyeenyeh
How much are the seats in the circle (balcony)?	Сколько стоят места в первом ярусе?	skol'kah stoyaht myehstah v pyehrvahm yahroossyeh

Opera—Ballet—Concert

There are more than 30 opera and ballet theatres in the USSR—
not just in Moscow and Leningrad, but in many other cities as
well. The Bolshoi Theatre, founded in 1776, has made Moscow
the capital of classical choreography. You should see your
Intourist representative about Bolshoi seats—even before leaving for the USSR. Despite its five tiers and a seating capacity
of 2,150, this world-renowned ballet theatre is usually sold out.

Where's the opera house?	Где оперный театр?	gdyeh **op**yeerniy tyee**ah**tr
What's on at the opera tonight?	Какая сегодня опера?	kah**kah**yah see**vod**nyah **op**yeerah
What's on at the ballet tonight?	Какой сегодня балет?	kah**koy** see**vod**nyah bah**lyeht**
What time does the performance start?	Когда начало?	kahg**dah** nah**chyah**lah
What orchestra is playing?	Какой оркестр играет?	kah**koy** ahr**kyehstr** ee**grah**eet
Who's the con- ductor?	Кто дирижирует?	kto dyeeree**zhi**rooeet
Who's the prima ballerina tonight?	Кто танцует главную партию?	kto tahn**tsoo**eet **glahv**nooyoo **pahr**tyeeyoo

Извините, все билеты проданы.

Осталось только несколько мест в первом ярусе.

Ваш билет, пожалуйста!

Вот ваше место.

I'm sorry, we're sold out.

There are only a few seats in the circle (balcony) left.

May I see your ticket?

This is your seat.

Nightclubs—Dancing

There's no such thing as a nightclub in the USSR. Cafés and restaurants where you can hear music and dance usually close at about midnight. On the other hand, you can hear singing and music in flats (apartments) until the wee hours of the morning.

Dances are held all year round in the recreation parks and are sponsored by youth organizations in clubs and "palaces of culture", as well as aboard ships and riverboats. Ask Intourist about this.

In restaurants where there's dancing, you can ask a girl for a dance, but you must ask the permission of the man accompanying her.

Where can we go dancing?	**Где можно потанце-вать?**	gdyeh **mozh**nah pahtahn-tsah**vaht'**
There's a dance at the palace of culture.	**В доме культуры вечер танцев.**	v **do**myeh kool'**too**ri **vyeh**chyehr **tahnt**sahv
I'd like to go to a Komsomol party.	**Я хотел бы пойти на комсомольский вечер.**	yah khah**tyehl** bi pigh**tyee** nah kahmsah**mol'**skeey **vyeh**chyehr
May I have this dance?	**Разрешите пригласить вас на танец.**	rahzree**shi**tyee preeglah-**sseet'**vahss nah **tah**-nyehts
Would you like to dance?	**Хотите потанцевать?**	khah**tyee**tyee pahtahntsah-**vaht'**
No, thanks, I don't feel like dancing.	**Нет, спасибо, мне не хочется.**	nyeht spah**ssee**bah mnyeh nyee **kho**chyeetsah

RELAXING

Do you happen to play …?

If you play chess in the Soviet Union, you're in. If you find Russian lessons a bore, bone up on chess before leaving for the USSR. A good game of chess will bring you closer to Russian people than your linguistic skills will. You might even take a mini-chess set along with you if you're planning a long train ride through the Soviet Union.

Do you happen to play chess?	Не играете ли вы случайно в шахматы?	nyee eegra**hee**tyee lyee vi sloochyigh**nah v shahkh**mahti
Sure, I do.	Да, конечно, играю.	dah kah**nyehsh**nah eegra**hyoo**
No, but I'll give you a game of draughts (checkers).	Нет, но мы могли бы сыграть в шашки.	nyeht no mi magh**lyee** bi sigra**ht v shahsh**kee
king	король	kah**rol'**
queen	ферзь	**fyehz'**
castle (rook)	ладья	lah**d'yah**
bishop	слон	slon
knight	конь	kon'
pawn	пешка	**pyehsh**kah
Do you play cards?	Вы играете в карты?	vi eegra**hee**tyee.v **kah**rti

The card games popular in the West are seldom played in Russia. But poker is a favourite among the intellectual set. Russians enjoy преферанс (pryeefyee**rahns**—preference) which somewhat resembles bridge. It's unusual for Russians to play cards in a café. On the other hand, card playing is common at the beach or on a long train ride.

Can you play preference?	Вы играете в преферанс?	vi eegra**hee**tyee v pryee-fyee**rahns**
ace	туз	tooz
king	король	kah**rol'**
queen	дама	**dah**mah
jack	валет	vah**lyeht**
joker	джокер	**dzho**kyehr

Sport

If you're fond of swimming, you can swim all year round in Moscow's enormous open-air, heated pool. There are quite a few members of the polar-bear club who swim in the Moscow River in freezing weather. Special holes must be cut in the ice.

Not exactly a sport is the Russian tradition of the баня (**bah-nyah**—sauna). This is a great way of restoring the soul and getting rid of fatigue. Burning hot stones are splashed with water at regular intervals and the steam can be unbearably hot. Then the naked bathers beat each other with birch branches. This is topped off by a quick plunge in a small pool of cold water.

I'd like to go to a swimming pool.	Где плавательный бассейн?	gdyeh **plah**vahtyehl'niy bah**ssyayn**
Is it heated?	Вода подогревается?	vah**dah** pahdahgryeh**vah**eetsah
Where is the nearest sauna?	Где ближайшая баня?	gdyeh blyee**zhigh**shchah-yah **bah**nyah
Can I check my clothes here?	Могу ли я здесь оставить одежду?	mah**goo** lyee yah zdyehs' ah**stah**veet' ah**dyehzh**doo
Give me a towel, please.	Дайте мне полотенце, пожалуйста.	**digh**tyee mnyeh pahlah-**tyehn**tseh pahzhah**loo**stah
Where are the tennis courts?	Где теннисная площадка?	gdyeh **teh**nyeesnahyah plah**shchyahd**kah
Can I hire rackets?	Можно взять ракетки напрокат?	**mozh**nah vzyaht' rah**kyeht**kee nahprah**kaht**
Is there a volley ball court here?	Есть ли здесь волей-больная площадка?	yehst' lyee zdyehs' vahlyeey-**bol**'nahyah plah**shchyahd**kah
Is there a football (soccer) match anywhere this Saturday?	Будет ли в эту субботу футбольный матч?	**boo**dyeet lyee v **eh**too soo**boo**too foot**bol**'niy mahhch'
Can you get me a couple of tickets?	Нельзя ли достать несколько билетов?	nyeel'**zyah** lyee dah**staht'** **nyeh**skahl'kah beel**yeh**tahv
Is there any good fishing around here?	Где здесь можно поудить рыбу?	gdyeh zdyehs' **mozh**nah pahoo**dyeet'** riboo

On the beach

Is it safe for swimming?	Здесь не опасно плавать?	zdyehs' nyee ahpahsnah plahvaht'
Is there a lifeguard?	Есть ли здесь спасательная команда?	yehst' lyee zdyehs' spahssahtyeel'nahyah kahmahndah
Is it safe for children?	Не опасно ли здесь для детей?	nyee ahpahsnah lyee zdyehs' dlyah dyeetyay
There are some big waves.	Бывают большие волны.	bivahyoot bahl'shiyeh volni
Are there any dangerous currents?	Есть ли опасные течения?	yehst' lyee ahpahsniyeh tyeechyehnyeeyah
You'd better not dive here.	Здесь лучше не нырять.	zdyehs' loochch'eh nyee niryaht'
What's the temperature of the water?	Какая температура воды?	kahkahyah tyeempyeerahtoorah vahdi
I want to hire…	Я хочу взять напрокат…	yah khahchyoo vzyaht' nahprahkaht
a beach chair	шезлонг	shehzlong
a sunshade	зонтик	zontyeek
a tent	тент	tyehnt
some water skis	водные лыжи	vodniyeh lizhi
Where can I rent…?	Где я могу взять напрокат…?	gdyeh yah mahgoo vzyaht' nahprahkaht
a canoe	каноэ	kahnoeh
a kayak	байдарку	bighdahrkoo
a rowing boat	лодку	lodkoo
an outboard motor boat	моторную лодку	mahtornooyoo lodkoo
a paddle boat	водяной велосипед	vahdyeenoy vyeelah-ssyeepyehd
a sailing boat	парусную лодку	pahroosnooyoo lodkoo
What's the charge per hour?	Сколько это стоит в час?	skol'kah ehtah stoeet v chyahss

---

КУПАТЬСЯ ВОСПРЕЩАЕТСЯ
NO SWIMMING

Winter sports

Skiing is becoming increasingly popular in the Soviet Union. If you want to make this one of the main features of your trip to the USSR, arrange to spend some time at a Soviet ski resort —let's say, in the Caucasus. However, it's possible to go skiing in the parks of Moscow and Leningrad, where you can also skate, go sledding, or take a troika ride. A few such places in Moscow are Gorky Park, Sokolniki Park and Izmaylovo Park.

I'd like to go ice skating.	Я хотел бы пока- таться на коньках.	yah khah**tyehl** bi pahkah- **tah**tsah nah kahn'**kahkh**
Is there a place nearby?	Далеко ли каток?	dahlyee**ko** lyee kah**tok**
I want to rent some skates.	Я хочу взять коньки напрокат.	yah khah**choo** vzyaht' kahn'**kee** nahprah**kaht**
What are the skiing conditions like at Sokolniki Park?	В «Сокольниках» хорошая лыжня?	v sahkol'nyeekahkh khah**ro**shahyah lizh**nyah**
The snow is a little soft.	Снег рыхловат.	snyehg rikhlah**vaht**
I'd like to do some cross-country skiing.	Я хотел бы пойти в лыжный поход.	yah khah**tyehl** bi pigh**tyee** v lizhniy pah**khod**
Can I take skiing lessons there?	Есть там школа для начинающих?	yehst' tahm **shko**lah dlyah nahchyee**nah**yooshchyeekh
Is there a ski lift?	Есть ли подъемник?	yehst' lyee pahd'**yom**neek
I want to rent skiing equipment.	Я хотел бы взять напрокат лыжный инвентарь.	yah khah**tyehl** bi vzyaht' nahprah**kaht** lizhniy eenvyehn**tahr**'
Can you help me adjust this binding?	Помогите мне, пожа- луйста, затянуть крепленье.	pahmah**ghee**tyee mnyeh pah**zhah**loostah zahtyah- **noot**' kryee**plehn**'yeh
Can I rent a sled?	Можно взять напрокат сани?	**mozh**nah vzyaht' nahprah- **kaht sah**nyee
Where can I take a troika ride?	Где можно пока- таться на тройке?	gdyeh **mozh**nah pahkah- **tah**tsah nah **troy**kyeh

Camping

In a country where hotel accommodation is fairly expensive, camping represents a real bargain, a way of making your money last the longest possible time. But you've got to have a car—no hitch-hiking or bicycle trips are allowed. You can rent a car or small bus at the border or you can drive in from some other country. Whatever the case may be, you'll have to set up an itinerary before going.

Can we camp here?	Можно здесь устроить стоянку?	mozhnah zdyehs' oostroeet' stahyahnkoo
Where can we camp for the night?	Где нам остановиться на ночь?	gdyeh nahm ahstahnah-veetsah nahnahch'
Is there a camping site near here?	Есть ли здесь недалёко кемпинг?	yehst' lyee zdyehs' nyee-dahlyokah kyehmpeeng
How far is it to Smolensk?	Сколько ехать до Смоленска?	skol'kah yehkhaht' dah smahlyehnskah
Are we on the right road for Kalinin?	Это дорога на Калинин?	ehtah dahrogah nah kah-lyeenyeen
Can we park our car here?	Можно здесь поставить машину?	mozhnah zdyehs' pahstahveet' mahshinoo
Where can I pitch my tent?	Где можно поставить палатку?	gdyeh mozhnah pahstah-veet' pahlahtkoo
What are the facilities?	Какие здесь удобства?	kahkeeyeh zdyehs' oodobstvah
I'd like to rent a beach hut.	Я хотел бы снять домик.	yah khahtyehl bi snyaht' domeek
May we light a fire?	Можно разжечь костёр?	mozhnah rahzzhehch' kahstyor

CAMPING

ПИТЬЕВАЯ ВОДА	DRINKING WATER
ВОДА НЕ ДЛЯ ПИТЬЯ	POLLUTED WATER

FOR CAMPING EQUIPMENT, see page 106

Intourist issues coupons for camping which you must use in paying for your camping site. Your travel arrangements comprise a place to pitch a tent (or use of a beach hut, if you choose) and a parking space for your car. There are many Soviet citizens at the camps, since they frequently hire cars and motorcycles with sidecars for touring the country. You can eat at the camp's snack-bar/restaurant or may ask to use the electric stoves provided for the use of the campers. Each camping site has a grocery store. Note that most camping sites are open only from June 1 to September 1.

If you forget to bring a tent, you may often be able to hire one from the camp staff for a moderate fee. The same holds true for folding cots, air mattresses, blankets and sleeping bags. Don't expect luxurious, modern plumbing in washrooms and toilets. Hot water may or may not be available.

What's the charge?	Сколько это стоит?	skol'kah ehtah stoeet
How many coupons do I owe you?	Сколько талонов я вам должен?	skol'kah tahlonahv yah vahm dolzhehn
May we use the electric stove?	Можно пользоваться электроплиткой?	mozhnah pol'zahvahtsah ehlyehktrahplyeetkigh
Where's the washroom?	Есть ли тут умывальник?	yehst' lyee toot oomivahl'nyeek
Where's the grocery store?	Где магазин?	gdyeh mahgahzeen
At what time does the grocery store open?	Когда открывается магазин?	kahgdah ahtkrivaheetsah mahgahzeen
Can we eat in the camp's restaurant?	Можно поесть в ресторане?	mozhnah pahyehst' v ryeestahrahnyeh
Is there a shower?	Есть ли здесь душ?	yehst' lyee zdyehs' doosh
Is there an iron?	Есть ли у вас утюг?	yehst' lyee oo vahss ootyoog

Landmarks

barn	амбар	ahm**bahr**
bridge	мост	most
brook	ручей	roo**chyay**
building	здание	**zdah**n'yeh
canal	канал	kah**nahl**
church	церковь	**tsehr**kahf'
cliff	обрыв	ah**briv**
collective farm	колхоз	kahl**khoz**
copse	роща	**ro**shchya
cornfield	поле	**po**lyeh
cottage	дача	**dah**chyah
farm	ферма	**fyehr**mah
ferry	паром	pah**rom**
field	поле	**po**lyeh
footpath	тропинка	trah**peen**kah
forest	лес	lyehss
hamlet	деревня	dyee**ryehv**nyah
hill	холм	kholm
house	дом	dom
inn	гостиница	gah**styee**nyeetsah
lake	озеро	**o**zyeerah
marsh	болото	bah**lo**tah
mountain	гора	gah**rah**
mountain range	горная цепь	**gor**nahyah tsehp
peak	пик	pyeek
plantation	плантация	plahn**tah**tsiyah
pond	пруд	prood
pool	заводь	**zah**vahd'
river	река	ryee**kah**
road	дорога	dah**ro**gah
spring	источник	ee**stoch**'nyeek
steppe	степь	styehp'
stream	река	ryee**kah**
swamp	болото	bah**lo**tah
taiga, swampy coniferous forest	тайга	tigh**gah**
track	просёлок	prah**ssyo**lahk
tree	дерево	**dyeh**ryeeevah
valley	долина	dah**lyee**nah
village	село	syee**lo**
vineyard	виноградник	veenah**grahd**nyeek
water	вода	vah**dah**
waterfall	водопад	vahdah**pahd**
well	колодец	kah**lo**dyeets
wood	лес	lyehss

Making friends

You'll find that many Soviet professional people and students have studied English. The Russians will be very eager to talk to you. They're just as excited about meeting a "real" Englishman or American as we are about seeing, hearing and rubbing shoulders with real Russians.

Introductions

When you get into a situation where an introduction is called for, you should bear in mind that forms like "Mr. Smith", "Mrs. Smith", "Miss Smith", just don't exist in everyday Russian. You'll have to know the first name and patronymic—which means the name derived from his or her father—of the person you're speaking to. If the Russian's Christian name is Nicholai and his father's name is Ivan, you'll address him as *Nicholai Ivanovich*. On the other hand, if it were a girl whose name is Natalia and whose father's name is Ivan, she'll be called *Natalia Ivanovna*.

Here are a few phrases to get you started.

How do you do?	Здравствуйте.	zdrahstvooytyee
How are you?	Как дела?	kahk dyeelah
Very well, thank you.	Очень хорошо, спасибо.	ochyeen' khahrahsho spahsseebah
How's it going?	Как дела?	kahk dyeelah
Fine, thanks. And you?	Хорошо, спасибо. А у вас?	khahrahsho spahsseebah. ah oo vahss

When referring to fellow Anglo-Saxons, it won't be wrong to use the words мисс (Miss), мистер (Mister) and миссис (Mrs.). Thus, we can say:

May I introduce Miss Phillips?	Позвольте представить вам мисс Филипс.	pahzvol'tyee pryeedstahveet' vahm Miss Phillips

Nicholai Ivanovich, this is Mr. Brown.	**Николай Иванович, это мистер Браун.**	nyeekahligh eevahnah-veech' ehtah Mister Brown
I'd like you to meet a friend of mine.	**Я хотел бы вас познакомить с одним из моих друзей.**	yah khahtyehl bi vahss pahznahkomeet' s ahdnyeem eez maheekh droozyay
John, this is ...	**Джон, это...**	John ehtah
My name's ...	**Меня зовут...**	myeenyah zahvoot
Delighted to meet you.	**Очень приятно.**	ochyeen' preeyahtnah
Glad to know you.	**Рад познакомиться.**	rahd pahznahkomeetsah

Note: For brief encounters, such as when asking directions, use the Soviet equivalent for "Mister" or "Miss". Thus, you'll say: "Excuse me, *tovarish*. Can you tell me where the bus is?" *Tovarish* (comrade—pronounced tah**vah**reeshch') can be used for both men and women. When speaking to a young girl, you'd say: "*Devushka*, where's the bus?" This word is pronounced **dyeh**vooshkah and means girl.

Follow-up

How long have you been here?	**Сколько вы уже здесь пробыли?**	skol'kah vi oozheh zdyehs' probilyee
We've been here a week.	**Мы тут уже неделю.**	mi toot oozheh nyeedyeh-lyoo
Is this your first visit?	**Вы в первый раз?**	vi v pyehrviy rahz
No, we came here last year.	**Нет, мы уже тут бы-ли в прошлом году.**	nyeht mi oozheh toot bilyee v proshlahm gahdoo
Are you enjoying your stay?	**Вам тут нравится?**	vahm toot nrahveetsah
Yes, I like ... very much.	**Да, мне...очень нравится.**	dah mnyeh ... ochyeen' nrahveetsah
Are you on your own?	**Вы одни?**	vi ahdnyee

I'm with…	Я с…	yah s
my wife	женой	zhinoy
my family	семьёй	syeem'yoy
my parents	родителями	rahdyeetyeelyahmee
some friends	друзьями	drooz'yahmyee
Where do you come from?	Вы откуда?	vi ahtkoodah
What part of … do you come from?	Вы из какой части…?	vi eez kahkoy chyahstyee
I'm from …	Я из…	yah eez
Do you live here?	Вы здесь живёте?	vi zdyehs' zhivyotyee
I'm a student.	Я студент.	yah stoodyehnt
What are you studying?	Что вы изучаете?	shto vi eezoochyaheetyee
We're here on holiday.	Мы здесь в отпуске.	mi zdyehs' v otpooskeh
I'm here on a business trip.	Я здесь по делам.	yah zdyehs' pah dyeelahm
What kind of business are you in?	Чем вы занимаетесь?	chyehm vi zahnyeemaheetyees'
I hope we'll see you again soon.	Надеюсь, мы скоро увидимся.	nahdyehyoos' mi skorah ooveedyeemsyah
See you later/ See you tomorrow.	До скорого/До завтра.	dah skorahvah/dah zahvtrah
I'm sure we'll run into each other again some time.	Я уверен, что мы еще встретимся.	yah oovyehryehn shto mi yeeshchyo vstryehtyeemsyah

MAKING FRIENDS

The weather

They talk about the weather just as much in the USSR as the British and Americans are supposed to do. So …

What a lovely day!	Какой чудный день!	kahkoy chyoodniy dyehn'
What awful weather.	Какая ужасная погода.	kahkahyah oozhahsnahyah pahgodah

Isn't it cold today?	Сегодня холодно, правда?	seevodnyah kholahdnah prahvdah
Isn't it hot today?	Сегодня жарко, правда?	seevodnyah zhahrkah prahvdah
Is it usually as warm as this?	Тут всегда так жарко?	toot vsyeegdah tahk zhahrkah
It's very foggy, isn't it?	Сегодня сильный туман.	seevodnyah **syeel**'niy **too**mahn
What's the temperature outside?	Сколько на улице градусов?	**skol**'kah nah **oo**lyeetseh **grah**doossahv

Invitations

My wife and I would like you to dine with us on …	Мы с женой хотим пригласить вас на ужин в …	mi s zhi**noy** khah**tyeem** preeglah**ssyeet**' vahss nah **oo**zhin v
Can you come to dinner tomorrow night?	Могли бы вы поужинать с нами завтра?	mahg**lyee** bi vi pah**oozhi**naht s **nah**mye **zahv**trah
We're giving a small party tomorrow night. I do hope you can come.	У нас завтра вечером гости. Я надеюсь, что вы придёте.	oo nahss **zahv**trah **vyeh**chyeerahm **gos**tyee. nah**dyeh**yooss shto vi pree**dyodyo**tye
Can you come round for cocktails this evening?	Не зайдёте ли вечером на коктейль?	nyee zighd**yo**tye lyee **vyeh**chyeerahm nah **kahk**tail'
There's a party. Are you coming?	Будут гости. Вы придёте?	**boo**doot **gos**tyee. vi pree**dyo**tye
That's very kind of you.	Большое спасибо.	bahl'**sho**yeh spah**ssyee**bah
Great. I'd love to come.	Замечательно! Приду с удовольствием.	zahmyee**chya**tyeel'nah! pree**doo** s oodah**vol**'st-veeyehm
What time shall we come?	В котором часу нам прийти?	v kah**to**rahm chyee**sso**o nahm pree**y**tye
May I bring a friend?	Можно привести приятеля?	**mozh**nah preevyees**tyee** pree**yah**tyeelyah
I'm afraid we've got to go now.	Пожалуй, нам пора.	pah**zhah**looy nahm pah**rah**

Next time you must come to visit us.	В следующий раз вы должны нас навестить.	v **slyeh**dooshchyeey rahz vi **dahl**zhni nahss nahvyees**tyeet'**
Thank you very much for an enjoyable evening.	Спасибо большое за приятный вечер.	spahs**see**bah bahl'**shoyeh** zah pree**yaht**niy **vyeh**chyeer
Thanks for the party. It was great.	Спасибо. Было замечательно!	spahs**see**bah. bilah zahmyee**chyah**tyeel'nah

Dating

Would you like a cigarette?	Не хотите ли сигарету?	nyee khat**yee**tyee lyee seegah**ryeh**too
Have you got a light, please?	Нет ли у вас спичек?	nyeht lyee oo vahss **speech**yehk
Can I get you a drink?	Хотите что-нибудь выпить?	khaht**yee**tyee **shton**yeebood' **vi**peet'
Excuse me, could you help me, please?	Простите, вы бы не могли мне помочь?	prahs**tyee**tyee vi bi nyee mahg**lyee** mnyeh pah**moch'**
I'm lost. Can you show me the way to…?	Я заблудился. Не покажете ли мне дорогу к…?	yah zahblood**yeel**syah. nyee pah**kah**zhityee lyee mneh dah**ro**goo k
Are you waiting for someone?	Вы кого-нибудь ждёте?	vi kah**von**yeebood' **zhdyot**yee
Are you free this evening?	Вы не заняты сегодня вечером?	vi nyee **zah**nyahti seevod**nyah vyeh**chyeerahm
Would you like to go out with me tonight?	Хотите, пойдём куда-нибудь сегодня вечером?	khaht**yee**tyee pighd**yom** koodah**nyee**bood' seevod**nyah vyeh**chyeerahm
Would you like to go dancing?	Не хотите ли потанцевать?	nyee khat**yee**tyee lyee pahtahntsah**vaht'**
I know a good restaurant.	Я знаю хороший ресторан.	yah **znah**yoo kha**ro**shiy ryeestah**rahn**
Shall we go to the cinema (movies)?	Давайте пойдём в кино.	dah**vigh**tyee pighd**yom** v **kee**no
Would you like to go for a drive?	Не хотите ли покататься на машине?	nyee khat**yee**tyee lyee pah**kah**tahtsah nah mah**shi**nyeh

I'd love to, thank you.	С удовольствием, спасибо.	s oodah**vol**'stveeyehm spah**ssee**bah
Where shall we meet?	Где мы встретимся?	gdyeh mi v**stryeh**tyeemsyah
I'll pick you up at your hotel.	Я зайду за вами в гостиницу.	yah zigh**doo** zah **vah**mee v gah**styee**nyeetsoo
I'll call for you at eight.	Я зайду за вами в восемь часов.	yah zigh**doo** zah **vah**mee v **vo**ssyeem' chyee**ssov**
May I take you home?	Можно вас проводить домой?	**mozh**nah vahss prahvah**dyeet**' dah**moy**
Can I see you again tomorrow?	Мы завтра встретимся?	mi **zah**vtrah v**stryeh**tyeemsyah
Thank you, it's been a wonderful evening.	Спасибо, я провёл чудесный вечер.	spah**ssee**bah yah prah**vyol** chyoo**dyes**niy **vyeh**chyeer
I've enjoyed myself tremendously.	Я получил громадное удовольствие!	yah pahloo**chyeel** grah**mahd**nahyeh oodah**vol**'-stveeyeh
What's your telephone number?	Какой у вас номер телефона?	kah**koy** oo vahss **no**myeer tyeelyeefo**nah**
Do you live with your family?	Вы живёте с родителями?	vi zhiv**yo**tyee s rah**dyee**tyeelyahmee
Do you live alone?	Вы живёте одни?	vi zhiv**yo**tyee ahd**nyee**
What time is your last train?	Когда ваш последний поезд?	kahg**dah** vahsh pah**slyehd**neey **po**eezd

Shopping guide

This shopping guide is designed to help you find what you want with ease, accuracy and speed. It features:

1. a list of all major shops, stores and services;

2. some general expressions required when shopping to allow you to be specific and selective;

3. full details of the shops and services most likely to concern you. Here you'll find advice, alphabetical lists of items and conversion charts listed under the headings below.

	Main items	Page
Bookshop	books, magazines, newspapers, stationery	104
Camping	camping equipment	106
Chemist's (drugstore)	medicine, first-aid, cosmetics, toilet articles	108
Clothing	clothes, shoes, accessories	112
Electrical appliances	radios, tape-recorders, razors, records	119
Hairdresser's	barber's, ladies' hairdresser's, beauty salon	121
Jeweller's	jewellery, watches, watch repairs	123
Laundry— Dry cleaning	usual facilities	126
Photography	cameras, accessories, films, developing	127
Provisions	this is confined to basic items required for picnics	129
Souvenirs	souvenirs, gifts, fancy goods	131
Tobacconist's	smoker's supplies	132

SHOPPING GUIDE

Shops, stores and services

If you've a pretty clear idea of what you want before you set out, do a little homework first. Look under the appropriate heading, pick out the article and find a suitable description for it (colour, material, etc.).

Shopping hours vary considerably. Most stores are open from 9 or 10 a.m. to 8 p.m., Monday to Saturday, some close for lunch. Certain shops—"Beriozka" stores—cater only to foreign tourists. They quote prices in rubles, but the goods must be paid for in hard currency. Quite a few of the items aren't available in ordinary shops. If you want to try shopping the way the Russians themselves do, visit one of the big department stores like GUM or TSUM in Moscow, or go to an outdoor market.

Where's the nearest...?	Где ближайший...?	gdyeh blyee**zhigh**shshchiy
antique shop	**антикварный магазин**	ahntyeek**vahr**niy mahgah**zeen**
art gallery	**картинная галерея**	kahr**teen**nahyah gahlyee-**ryeh**yah
baker's	**булочная**	**boo**lahshnahyah
bank	**банк**	bahnk
barber's	**парикмахерская**	pahreek**mahk**hyeerskahyah
beauty salon	**косметический кабинет**	kahsmyee**tyee**chyeeskeey kahbee**nyeht**
bookshop	**книжный магазин**	**kneezh**niy mahgah**zeen**
butcher's	**мясной магазин**	myahs**noy** mahgah**zeen**
camera store	**магазин кино- и фотоаппаратуры**	mahgah**zeen** keenah- ee fotahahpahrah**too**ri
candy store	**кондитерская**	kahn**dyee**tyeerskahyah
chemist's	**аптека**	ahp**tyeh**kah
cigar store	**табачный магазин**	tah**bahch'**niy mahgah**zeen**
dairy shop	**молочная**	mah**losh**nahyah
delicatessen	**гастроном**	gahstrah**nom**
dentist	**зубной врач**	zoob**noy** vrahch'
department store	**универмаг**	oonyeevyehr**mahg**
doctor	**врач**	vrahch'
dressmaker's	**ателье дамского платья**	ahtehl'**yeh dahm**skahvah **plaht'**yah
drugstore	**аптека**	ahp**tyeh**kah
dry cleaner's	**химчистка**	kheem**chyeest**kah

fishmonger's	**рыбный магазин**	**rib**niy mahgah**zeen**
florist's	**цветочный магазин**	tsvyee**toch'**niy mahgah**zeen**
furrier's	**меховой магазин**	myeekhah**voy** mahgah**zeen**
greengrocer's	**овощной магазин**	ahvahshch'**noy** mahgah-**zeen**
grocery	**бакалея**	bahkah**lyeh**yah
hairdresser's (ladies)	**дамская парик-махерская**	**dahm**skahyah pahreek-**mahkh**yeerskahyah
hardware store	**скобяной магазин**	skahbyah**noy** mahgah**zeen**
hat shop	**магазин головных уборов**	mahgah**zeen** gahlahv**nikh** ooborahv
hospital	**больница**	bahl'**nyee**tsah
ironmonger's	**скобяной магазин**	skahbyah**noy** mahgah**zeen**
jeweller's	**ювелирный магазин**	yoovyee**lyeer**niy mahgah-**zeen**
laundry	**прачечная**	**prah**chyeeshnahyah
liquor store	**винный магазин**	**veen**niy mahgah**zeen**
market	**рынок**	**ri**nahk
milliner's	**ателье дамских шляп**	ahtehl'**yeh dahm**skeekh shlyahp
news-stand	**газетный киоск**	gah**zyeht**niy kee**osk**
off-licence	**винный магазин**	**veen**niy mahgah**zeen**
optician	**изготовленье и продажа очков**	eezgahtahv**lehn'**yeh ee prah**dah**zhah ahch'**kov**
pastry shop	**кондитерская**	kahn**dyeet**yeerskahyah
photographer's	**фотография**	fahtah**grah**feeyah
photo shop	**магазин фототоваров**	mahgah**zeen** fotahtah-**vah**rahv
police station	**отделение милиции**	ahtdyee**lyehn'**yeh mee**lyee**tsiee
post-office	**почта**	**poch'**tah
shoemaker's (repairs)	**ремонт обуви**	ryee**mont** oboovyee
shoe shop	**магазин обуви**	mahgah**zeen** oboovyee
souvenir shop	**магазин сувениров**	mahgah**zeen** soovyeh-**nyee**rahv
stamp collector's shop	**магазин марок**	mahgah**zeen mah**rahk
sweet shop	**кондитерская**	kahn**dyeet**yeerskahyah
tailor's	**ателье мод**	ahtehl'**yeh** mod
tobacconist's	**табачный магазин**	tah**bahch'**niy mahgah**zeen**
toy shop	**магазин игрушек**	mahgah**zeen** eegroo**shehk**
veterinarian	**ветеринар**	vyehtyehree**nahr**
watchmaker's	**часовая мастерская**	chyahsah**vah**yah mah-**styeer**skahyah
wine merchant's	**винный магазин**	**veen**niy mahgah**zeen**

General expressions

Here are some expressions which will be useful to you when you're out shopping.

Where?

Where's a good…?	Где хороший…?	gdyeh khah**ro**shiy
Where's the nearest…?	Где ближайший…?	gdyeh blyee**zhigh**shiy
Where can I find a…?	Где мне найти…?	gdyeh mnyeh nigh**tyee**
Can you recommend an inexpensive…?	Могли бы вы мне посоветовать дешёвый…?	mah**glyee** bi vi mnyeh pahssah**vyeh**tahvaht' dyee**sho**viy
Where's the main shopping centre?	Где главный торговый центр?	gdyeh **glahv**niy tahr**go**viy tsehntr
How do I get there?	Как мне туда попасть?	kahk mnyeh too**dah** pah**pahst'**

Service

Can you help me?	Будьте добры!	**boot'**tyee dahb**ri**
I'm just looking around.	Я только смотрю.	yah **tol'**kah smah**tryoo**
I want…	Я хочу…	yah khah**chyoo**
Can you show me some…?	Покажите мне, пожалуйста…	pahkah**zhi**tyee mnyeh pah**zhah**loostah
Have you any…?	Есть ли у вас…?	yehst' lyee oo vahss

That one

Can you show me…?	Покажите мне, пожалуйста,…	pahkah**zhi**tyee mnyeh pah**zhah**loostah
that/those	этот/те	tot/tyeh
the one in the window	тот в витрине	tot v vee**tree**nyeh
the one in the display case	тот, который выставлен	tot kah**to**riy **vi**stahvlyehn
It's over there.	Это там.	**eh**tah tahm

Defining the article

| I'd like a… | Я хотел бы… | yah khah**tyehl** bi |
| I want a … one. | Я хочу… | yah khah**chyoo** |

big	большой	bahl'**shoy**
cheap	дешёвый	dyee**shoviy**
dark	тёмный	**tyom**niy
good	хороший	khah**roshiy**
heavy	тяжёлый	tyee**zholiy**
large	крупный	**kroop**niy
light (weight)	лёгкий	**lyokh**keey
light (colour)	светлый	**svyeht**liy
oval	овальный	ah**vahl'**niy
rectangular	прямоугольный	pryahmahoo**gol'**niy
round	круглый	**kroog**liy
small	маленький	**mahl**yeen'keey
square	квадратный	kvahd**raht**niy

| I don't want any-thing too expensive. | Я не хочу ничего слишком дорогого. | yah nyee khah**chyoo** nyeechyee**vo slyeesh**kahm dahrah**go**vah |

Preference

Can you show me some more?	Покажите мне, пожалуйста, ещё.	pahkah**zhi**tyee mnyeh pah-**zhah**loostah yee**shchyo**
Haven't you any-thing…?	Есть ли у вас что-нибудь…	yehst' lyee oo vahss **shton**yeebood'
cheaper/better	подешевле/получше	pahdyee**shehv**lyee/pah-**looch**sheh
larger/smaller	побольше/поменьше	pah**bol'**sheh/pah**myehn'**-sheh

How much?

How much is this?	Сколько это стоит?	**skol'**kah **eh**tah **sto**eet
I don't understand. Please write it down.	Я не понимаю. Напишите это, по-жалуйста.	yah nyee pahnyee**mah**yoo. nah**pee**shi**tyee eh**tah pah-**zhah**loostah
I don't want to spend more than … rubles.	Я не хочу истратить больше… рублей.	yah nyee khah**chyoo** eestrah**tyeet' bol'**sheh …roo**blyay**

FOR COLOURS, see page 113

Decision

That's just what I want.	Это как раз то, что я хочу.	**ehtah** kahk rahz to shto yah khah**chyoo**
It's not quite what I want.	Это не совсем то, что я хочу.	**ehtah** nyee sahv**syehm** to shto yah khah**chyoo**
No, I don't like it.	Нет, мне это не нравится.	nyeht mnyeh **ehtah** nyee **nrah**veetsah
I'll take it.	Я это возьму.	yah **ehtah** vahz'**moo**

Ordering

Can you order it for me?	Будьте добры, закажите.	**boot'**tyee dah**bri** zahkah-**zhityee**
How long will it take?	Сколько это займёт?	skol'kah **ehtah** zigh**myot**
I'd like it as soon as possible.	Как можно быстрее, пожалуйста.	kahk **mozhnah** bi**stryeh**hyeh pah**zhah**loostah
Will I have any difficulty with customs?	Будут ли у меня трудности на таможне?	**boodoot** lyee oo myee-**nyah troodnahs**tyee nah tah**mozhnyeh**

Paying

How much is it?	Сколько это стоит?	skol'kah **ehtah stoeet**
Can I pay by travel-ler's cheque?	Вы берёте дорожные чеки?	vi byeh**ryotyee** dah**rozh**niyeh **chyehkee**
Do you accept credit cards?	Вы берёте кредит-ные карточки?	vi byeh**ryotyee** kryeh-**dyeet**niyeh **kahr**tahch'kee
Haven't you made a mistake in the bill?	Вы не ошиблись в счёте?	vi nyee ah**shiblyees'** v **shchyotyeh**
Can I have a receipt, please?	Будьте добры, чек.	**boot'**tyee dah**bri** chyehk
Will you wrap it, please?	Заверните, пожа-луйста.	zahvyeer**nyee**tyee pah**zhah**loostah
Have you got a carrier (shopping) bag?	Есть ли у вас сумка?	yehst' lyee oo vahss **soom**kah

Anything else?

No, thanks, that's all.	Нет, спасибо, это всё.	nyeht spahsseebah ehtah vsyo
Let me see— I want…	Дайте мне подумать. Я хотел бы…	dightyee mnyeh pahdoomaht'. yah khahtyehl bi
Yes, I want…/ Show me…	Да, я хочу…/Покажите мне…	dah yah khahchyoo…/ pahkahzhityee mnyeh
Thank you. Goodbye.	Спасибо. До свидания.	spahsseebah. dah sveedahn'yah

Dissatisfied

Can you exchange this, please?	Нельзя ли это обменять?	nyeel'zyah lyee ehtah ahbmyeenyaht'
I want to return this.	Я хочу это возвратить.	yah khahchyoo ehtah vahzvrahtyeet'
I'd like a refund. Here's the receipt.	Я хотел бы получить деньги обратно. Вот чек.	yah khahtyehl bi pahloochyeet' dyehn'ghee ahbrahtnah. vot chyehk

Пожалуйста, слушаю вас.		Can I help you?
Что бы вы хотели?		What would you like?
Какой … вы хотите?		What … would you like?
цвет/размер качество/количество		colour/shape quality/quantity
Извините, этого у нас нет.		I'm sorry, we haven't any.
Всё распродано.		We're out of stock.
Заказать для вас?		Shall we order it for you?
… рублей, пожалуйста.		That's … rubles, please.
Касса там.		The cashier's over there.

Bookshop—Stationer's—News-stand

In the USSR, bookshops and stationers' are usually separate shops. Magazines and newspapers are sold at news-stands.

Where's the nearest ...?	Где ближайший ...?	gdyeh blyeezhighshchiy
bookshop	книжный магазин	knyeezhniy mahgahzeen
stationer's	писчебумажный магазин	peeshchyehboomahzhniy mahgahzeen
news-stand	газетный киоск	gahzyehtniy keeosk
Where can I buy an English newspaper?	Где мне купить английскую газету?	gdyeh mnyeh koopeet' ahngleeyskooyoo gahzyehtoo
I want to buy a/an/some ...	Я хотел бы купить ...	yah khahtyehl bi koopeet'
address book	записную книжку для адресов	zahpeesnooyoo knyeezhkoo dlyah ahdryeessov
ball-point pen	шариковую ручку	shahreekahvooyoo rooch'koo
book	книгу	knyeegoo
box of paints	краски	krahskee
carbon paper	копировальную бумагу	kahpeerahvahl'nooyoo boomahgoo
crayons	карандаши	kahrahndahshi
dictionary	словарь	slahvahr'
Russian-English	русско-английский	rooskah ahngleeyskeey
English-Russian	англо-русский	ahnglah rooskeey
pocket dictionary	карманный словарь	kahrmahnniy slahvahr'
drawing paper	бумагу для рисования	boomahgoo dlyah reessahvahn'yah
drawing pins	чертёжные кнопки	chyeertyozhniyeh knopkee
envelopes	конверты	kahnvyehrti
eraser	резинку	reezeenkoo
file	скоросшиватель	skorahshshivahtyehl'
fountain pen	авторучку	ahvtahrooch'koo
glue	клей	klyay
grammar book	учебник	oochyehbnyeek
guide book	путеводитель	pootyeevahdyeetyehl'
ink	чернила	chyeernyeelah
black/red/blue	чёрные/красные/синие	chyorniyeh/krahsniyeh/seenyeeyeh
magazine	журнал	zhoornahl
map	план	plahn
map of the town	план города	plahn gorahdah

road map	карту дорог	**kahr**too dah**rog**
newspaper	газету	gah**zyeht**oo
American	американскую	ahmyeeree**kahn**skooyoo
English	английскую	ahn**glyeey**skooyoo
notebook	записную книжку	zahpees**noo**yoo **knyeezh**-koo
note paper	почтовую бумагу	pahch'**to**vooyoo **boo**mahgoo
paper napkins	бумажные салфетки	boo**mahzh**niyeh sahl**fyeht**-kee
pen	ручку	**rooch'**koo
pencil	карандаш	kahrahn**dahsh**
pencil sharpener	точилку	tah**chyeel**koo
refill (for a pen)	чернила для авторучки	chyeer**nyee**lah dlyah ahvtah**rooch'**kyee
rubber bands	резинки	ree**zeen**kee
ruler	линейку	lyee**nyay**koo
string	бечёвку	byee**chyov**koo
thumb tacks	чертёжные кнопки	chyeer**tyozh**niyeh **knop**kee
tracing paper	кальку	**kahl'**koo
typewriter ribbon	ленту для пишущей машинки	**lyehn**too dlyah **pee**shoo-shchyay mah**shin**kee
typing paper	бумагу для машинки	**boo**mahgoo dlyah mah-**shin**kee
wrapping paper	обёрточную бумагу	ah**byor**tahch'nooyoo **boo**mahgoo
writing pad	блокнот	blahk**not**
Where's the guide-book section?	Где отдел путеводителей?	gdyeh ahtdyehl pootyee-vah**dyee**tyeelyay
Where do you keep the English books?	Где у вас английские книги?	gdyeh oo vahss ahn-**glyeey**skeeyeh **knyee**ghee
Is there an English translation of ...?	Есть ли по-английски...?	yehst' lyee pah-ahn**glyeey**-skee

Camping

Here we're concerned with the equipment you may need.

I'd like a/an/some…	Я хотел бы купить…	yah khah**tyehl** bi koo**peet'**
axe	топор	tah**por**
bottle-opener	открывалку для бутылок	ahtkri**vahl**koo dlyah boo**ti**lahk
bucket	ведро	vyee**dro**
butane gas	газ в баллонах	gahz v bah**lo**nahkh
camp bed	складную кровать	sklahd**noo**yoo krah**vaht'**
camping equipment	оборудование для лагеря	ahbah**roo**dahvahn'yeh dlyah **lahg**heeryah
can opener	консервный нож	kahn**syehrv**niy nozh
candles	свечки	**svyehch'**kee
chair	стул	stool
folding chair	складной стул	sklahd**noy** stool
compass	компас	**kom**pahss
corkscrew	штопор	**shto**pahr
crockery	посуду	pahs**soo**doo
cutlery	ножи, вилки, ложки	nah**zhi vee**lkee **lozh**kee
deck chair	шезлонг	shehz**long**
first-aid kit	набор «первая помощь»	nah**bor** pyeh**r**vahyah **po**mahshch'
fishing tackle	рыболовные снасти	ribah**lov**niyeh **snah**styee
flashlight	карманный фонарик	kahr**mah**nniy fah**nah**reek
frying pan	сковородку	skahvah**rod**koo
groundsheet	подстилку под палатку	pahd**steel**koo pahd pah**lah**tkoo
hammer	молоток	mahl**lah**tok
hammock	гамак	gah**mahk**
haversack	сумку с лямкой	**soom**koo s **lyahm**kigh
ice-bag	пузырь для льда	poo**zir'** dlyah l'dah
kerosene	керосин	kyeerah**sseen**
kettle	чайник	**chy**ighnyeek
knapsack	рюкзак	ryook**zahk**
lamp	лампу	**lahm**poo
lantern	фонарь	fah**nahr'**
matches	спички	**speech'**kee
mattress	матрас	mah**trahss**
mosquito net	сетку от комаров	**syeht**koo aht kahmah**rov**
paraffin	керосин	kyeerah**sseen**
penknife	перочинный ножик	pyeerah**chyeen**niy **no**zhik
pressure cooker	герметическую кастрюлю	ghyehrmeh**tyee**chyehskoo-yoo kah**stryoo**lyoo

primus stove	примус	**pree**mooss
rope	верёвку	vyeh**ryov**koo
rucksack	рюкзак	ryook**zahk**
saucepan	кастрюлю	kah**stryoo**lyoo
scissors	ножницы	**nozh**nyeetsi
screwdriver	отвертку	aht**vyort**koo
sleeping bag	спальный мешок	**spahl**'niy myee**shok**
stewpan	кастрюлю	kah**stryoo**lyoo
stove	печку	**pyehch**'koo
table	стол	stol
folding table	складной стол	sklah**dnoy** stol
tent	палатку	pah**laht**koo
tent pegs	палаточные колышки	pah**laht**ahch'niyeh **ko**lishkee
tent-pole	палаточный столб	pah**laht**ahch'niy stolb
thermos flask (bottle)	термос	**tehr**mahss
tin-opener	консервный нож	kahn**syehrv**niy nozh
tongs	клещи	**klyeh**shchyee
tool kit	набор инструментов	**nahb**or eenstroo**myehn**tahv
torch	карманный фонарик	kahr**mahn**niy fah**nah**reek
vacuum flask (bottle)	термос	**tehr**mahss
water carrier (jug)	бак для воды	bahk dlyah vah**di**

Crockery

cups	чашки	**chyahsh**kee
food box	коробка для еды	kah**robkah** dlyah yeh**di**
mugs	кружки	**kroozh**kee
plates	тарелки	tah**ryehl**kee
saucers	блюдца	**blyood**tsah

Cutlery

forks	вилки	**veel**kee
knives	ножи	**nah**zhi
dessert knife	десертный нож	dyeh**ssyehrt**niy nozh
spoons	ложки	**lozh**kee
teaspoons	чайные ложки	**chigh**niyeh **lozh**kee
(made of) plastic	пластмасса	plah**stmah**ssah
(made of) stainless steel	нержавеющая сталь	nyeerzhah**vyeh**yoo-shchyahyah stahl'

Chemist's (pharmacy)—Drugstore

For medicine of any kind, you must go to an **аптека** (ahp**tyeh**-kah). Soviet chemists' don't stock the great range of goods that you find in England or the United States. Unlike medical treatment (which is free in the Soviet Union), you'll have to pay for anything that you buy at the chemist's. There's usually a sign in the window telling you where the nearest all-night chemist's is located.

For reading ease, this section has been divided into two parts:

1. Pharmaceutical—medicine, first-aid, etc.
2. Toiletry—toilet articles, cosmetics.

General

Where's the nearest (all-night) chemist's?	Где ближайшая дежурная аптека?	gdyeh blyee**zhigh**shahyah dyee**zhoor**nahyah ahp**tyeh**kah
What time does the chemist's open/close?	В котором часу от-крывается/закрывается аптека?	v kaht**o**rahm chyee**esso**o ahtkriva**hee**tsah/zahkri-**vah**eetsah ahp**tyeh**kah

Part 1—Pharmaceutical

I want something for...	Дайте мне, пожалуй-ста, что-нибудь от...	**digh**tyee mnyeh pah**zhah**-loostah **sht**onyeebood' aht
a cold/a cough hay fever	простуды/кашля сенной лихорадки	prah**stoo**di/**kahsh**lyah syehn**noy** lyeekhahrahd-kee
sunburn travel sickness	солнечного ожога морской болезни	s**o**lnyeech'nahvah ah**zho**gah mahr**skoy** bah**lyehz**nyee
Can you make me up this prescription?	Вы можете пригото-вить это лекарство?	vi m**o**zhityee preegaht**o**-veet' ehtah leekahrstvah
Shall I wait?	Мне подождать?	mnyeh pahdah**zhdaht'**
When shall I come back?	Когда мне вернуться?	kahg**dah** mnyeh vyeer**noo**-tsah

FOR DOCTOR, see page 162

Can I get it without a prescription?	Можно получить это без рецепта?	mozhnah pahloochyeet' ehtah byehz reetsehptah
Can I have a/an/ some ...?	Дайте мне, пожалуй- ста...	dightyee mnyeh pahzhah- loostah
ammonia	нашатырный спирт	nahshahtirniy speert
antiseptic cream	антисептическую мазь	ahntyeesyehptyeechyeh- skooyoo mahz'
aspirin	аспирин	ahspeereen
bandage	гигиенический бинт	gheegheeyehnyeechyehs- keey beent
gauze bandage	марлевый бинт	mahrlyehviy beent
Band-aids	пластырь	plahstir
castor oil	касторовое масло	kahstorahvahyeh mahslah
contraceptives (male)	презервативы	preezyeervahtyeevi
corn plasters	мозольный пластырь	mahzol'niy plahstir'
cotton wool	вату	vahtoo
cough lozenges	таблетки от кашля	tahblyehtkee aht kahshlyah
diabetic lozenges	таблетки от сахарной болезни	tahblyehtkee aht sahkhahr- nigh bahlyehznyee
disinfectant	дезинфицирующее средство	dyehzeenfeetsirooyoo- shchyehyeh sryehdstvah
ear drops	ушные капли	ooshniyeh kahplyee
Elastoplast	пластырь	plahstir'
eye drops	глазные капли	glahzniyeh kaplyee
gargle	полоскание для горла	pahlahskahn'yeh dlyah gorlah
gauze	марлю	mahrlyoo
insect repellent	средство от комаров	sryehdstvah aht kahmahrov
iodine	йод	yod
laxative	слабительное	slahbeetyeel'nahyeh
mouthwash	полоскание для рта	pahlahskahn'yeh dlyah rtah
sanitary napkins	гигиенические салфетки	gheegheeyehnyeechyehs- keeyeh sahlfyehtkee
sedative	успокаивающее	oospahkaheevahyoo- shchyehyeh
sleeping pills	снотворное	snahtvornahyeh
stomach pills	таблетки для желудка	tahblyehtkee dlyah zhiloodkah
thermometer	термометр	tyeermomyehtr
throat lozenges	таблетки для горла	tahblyehtkee dlyah gorlah
vitamin pills	витамины	veetahmeeni

Part 2—Toiletry

SHOPPING GUIDE

I'd like a/an/some…	Дайте мне, пожалуйста…	dightyee mnyeh pahzhahloostah
acne cream	мазь от прыщей	mahz' ot prishchyay
after-shave lotion	одеколон после бритья	ahdyeekahlon poslyeh breet'yah
astringent	средство, стягивающее кожу	sryehdstvah styahghee-vahyooshchyehyeh kozhoo
bath essence	пенящуюся жидкость для ванны	pyehnyahshchyooyoossyah zhidkahst' dlyah vahnni
bath salts	экстракт для ванны	ehkstrahkt dlyah vahnni
cologne	одеколон	ahdyeekahlon
cream	крем	kryehm
cleansing cream	крем для снятия косметики	kryehm dlyah snyaht'yah kahsmyehtyeekee
cold cream	кольдкрем	kol'dkryehm
foundation cream	крем-тон	kryehm-ton
hormone cream	гормональный крем	gahrmahnahl'niy kryehm
moisturizing cream	жирный крем	zhirniy kryehm
night cream	ночной крем	nahch'noy kryehm
deodorant	средство от пота	sryehdstvah aht potah
eye pencil	карандаш для глаз	kahrahndash dlyah glahz
eye shadow	краску для глаз	krahskoo dlyah glahz
face powder	пудру	poodroo
hand cream	крем для рук	kryehm dlyah rook
lipstick	губную помаду	goobnooyoo pahmahdoo
make-up bag	сумочку для косметики	soomahch'koo dlyah kahsmyehtyeekee
nail brush	щёточку для ногтей	shchyotahch'koo dlyah nahgtyay
nail clippers	кусачки	koossahch'kee
nail file	пилочку	pyeelahch'koo
nail lacquer	лак для ногтей	lahk dlyah nahgtyay
nail scissors	ножницы для ногтей	nozhnyeetsi dlyah nahgtyay
oil	масло	mahslah
perfume	духи	dookhee
powder	пудру	poodroo
powder puff	пуховку	pookhovkoo
razor blades	лезвия	lyehzveeyah
rouge	румяна	roomyahnah
cream/powder	крем/пудру	kryehm/poodroo
shampoo	шампунь	shahmpoon'
liquid	жидкий	zhidkeey

shaving brush	кисточку для бритья	**kees**tahch'koo dlyah breet'**yah**
shaving cream	крем для бритья	kryehm dlyah breet'**yah**
shaving soap	мыло для бритья	**mi**lah dlyah breet'**yah**
soap	мыло	**mi**lah
sun-tan cream	крем для загара	kryehm dlyah zah**gah**rah
sun-tan oil	масло для загара	**mahs**lah dlyah zah**gah**rah
talcum powder	тальк	tahl'k
tissues	бумажные салфетки	boo**mahzh**niyeh sahl-**fyeht**kee
toilet paper	туалетную бумагу	tooah**lyeht**nooyoo boo-**mah**goo
toilet water	одеколон	ahdyeekah**lon**
toothbrush	зубную щётку	zoob**noo**yoo **shchyot**koo
toothpaste	зубную пасту	zoob**noo**yoo **pahs**too
towel	полотенце	pahlah**tyehn**tseh

For your hair

brush	щётка	**shchyot**kah
colouring	краска	**krahs**kah
comb	гребень	**grehb**yehn'
curlers	бигуди	beegoo**dyee**
dye/tint	краска/оттенок	**krahs**kah/ah**tty eh**nahk
grips (bobby pins)	заколки	zah**kol**kee
lacquer	лак	lahk
pins	шпильки	**shpeel'**kee

For the baby

beaker (tumbler)	чашка	**chyash**kah
bib	детский нагрудник	**dyehts**keey nah**grood**nyeek
dummy (pacifier)	соска (пустышка)	**sos**kah (**poo**stishkah)
food	еда	yeh**dah**
nappies (diapers)	пелёнки	pyee**lyon**kee
nappy pins	английские булавки	ahn**glee**yskeeyeh boo**lahv**kee
oil sheet	клеёнка	klyeeyon**kah**

Note: Many toiletry and cosmetic articles, common in the West, aren't manufactured in the USSR.

SHOPPING GUIDE

Clothing

If you want to buy something specific, prepare yourself in advance. Look at the list of clothing on page 117. Get some idea of the colour, material and size you want. They're all listed in the next few pages.

General

I'd like …	Я хотел бы…	yah khah**tyel** bi
I want … for a 10-year-old boy.	Мне нужен… для десятилетнего мальчика.	mnyeh **noo**zhin … dlyah dyeessyahtyee**lyeh**tnyeevah **mahl**'chyeekah
I want something like this.	Мне нужно что-нибудь вроде этого.	mnyeh **noo**zhnah **shto**-nyeebood' **vro**dyeh **eh**tahvah
How much is that per metre?	Сколько стоит метр?	**skol**'kah **sto**eet myehtr

1 centimetre = 0.39 in.		1 inch = 2.54 cm.
1 metre = 39.37 in.		1 foot = 30.5 cm.
10 metres = 32.81 ft.		1 yard = 0.91 m.

Colour

I want something in …	Мне нужно что-нибудь…	mnyeh **noo**zhnah **shto**-nyeebood'
I want a darker shade.	Мне нужно что-нибудь потемнее.	mnyeh **noo**zhnah **shto**-nyeebood' pahtyeem-**nyeh**yeh
I want something to match this.	Мне нужно что-нибудь в тон к этому.	mnyeh **noo**zhnah **shto**-nyeebood' v ton k **eh**tahmoo
I don't like the colour.	Мне этот цвет не нравится.	mnyeh **eh**taht tsvyeht nyee **nrah**veetsah

beige	бéж	byehzh
black	чёрный	**chyor**niy
blue	синий	**see**nyeey
brown	коричневый	kah**reesh**nyeeviy
cream	кремовой	**kryeh**mahviy
crimson	малиновый	mah**lyee**nahviy
emerald	изумрудный	eezoom**rood**niy
fawn	желтовато-коричневый	zhiltah**vah**tah-kah**reesh**-nyeeviy
gold	золотого цвета	zahlah**to**vah tsvyehtah
green	зелёный	zyee**lyo**niy
grey	серый	**syeh**riy
mauve	сиреневый	seer**yehn**yeeviy
orange	оранжевый	ah**rahn**zhiviy
pink	розовый	**ro**zahviy
purple	пурпурный	poor**poor**niy
red	красный	**krahs**niy
silver	серебряный	syeer**yehb**ryehniy
tan	рыжевато-коричневый	rizhi**vah**tah-kah**reesh**-nyeeviy
white	белый	**byeh**liy
yellow	жёлтый	**zhol**tiy

в полоску
(v pah**los**koo)

в горошек
(v gah**ro**shik)

в клетку
(v **klyeh**tkoo)

с узором
(s oo**zo**rahm)

Material

Have you anything in …?	Есть у вас что-нибудь…?	yehst' oo vahss **shto**-nyeebood'
Is that made here?	Это здешнее производство?	**eh**tah z**dyehsh**nyeyeh pra**heez**vodstvah
hand-made	ручное производство	rooch**no**yeh pra**heezvod**stvah
imported	импортное	eem**pahrt**nyahyeh
I want something thinner.	Мне нужно что-нибудь потоньше.	mnyeh **noozh**nah **shto**-nyeebood' pah**ton'**sheh
Have you any better quality?	Есть ли у вас что-нибудь лучшего качества?	yehst' lyee oo vahss **shto**-nyeebood' **looch**shivah **kah**chyehstvah

What's it made of?	Какой это материал?	kah**koy eh**tah mahtyee-r'**yahl**

It may be made of …

cambric	(из) батиста	(eez) bah**tyees**tah
corduroy	вельвета	vyehl'**vyeh**tah
cotton	бумажной ткани	boomah**zh**nigh **tkah**nyee
felt	фетра	**fyeht**rah
flannel	фланели	flah**neh**lyee
gabardine	габардина	gahbahr**dyee**nah
lace	кружева	kroo**zhi**vah
leather	кожи	**kozh**i
linen	полотна	pahlaht**nah**
nylon	нейлона	nyee**ylo**nah
poplin	поплина	pah**ply**eenah
rayon	искусственного шёлка	ees**koost**vyeennahvah **shol**kah
rubber	резины	ry**eezee**ni
satin	атласа	ah**tlahss**ah
serge	саржи	**sahrzh**i
silk	шёлка	**shol**kah
suede	замши	**zahm**shi
taffeta	тафты	tah**fti**
towelling	махровой ткани	mah**khro**vigh **tkah**nyee
tulle	тюля	**tyool**yah
tweed	твида	**tvee**dah
velvet	бархата	**bahr**khahtah
velveteen	вельветина	vyehl'**vyeh**tyeenah
wool	шерсти	**shehrs**tyee
worsted	шерсти	**shehrs**tyee

Size

My size is 38.	Мой размер 38.	moy rahz**myehr** 38
Our sizes are different at home. Could you measure me.	У нас другие размеры. Нельзя ли снять с меня мерку?	oo nahs droo**ghee**yeh rahz**myehr**i. nyeel'**zyah** lyee snyaht' s myee**nyah myehr**koo
I don't know the Russian sizes.	Я не знаю русских размеров.	yah nyee **znah**yoo **roos**keekh rahz**myehr**ahv

In that case, look at the charts on the next page.

This is your size

Ladies

Dresses/suits					
American	10	12	14	16	18	20
British	32	34	36	38	40	42
Russian	38	40	42	44	46	48

Stockings						Shoes			
American ⎫	8	8½	9	9½	10	10½	6	7	8	9
British ⎭							4½	5½	6½	7½
Russian	0	1	2	3	4	5	36	37	38½	40

Gentlemen

Suits/overcoats						Shirts			
American ⎫	36	38	40	42	44	46	15	16	17	18
British ⎭										
Russian	46	48	50	52	54	56	38	41	43	45

Shoes									
American ⎫	5	6	7	8	8½	9	9½	10	11
British ⎭									
Russian	38	39	41	42	43	43	44	44	45

A good fit?

Can I try it on?	**Можно примерить?**	mozhnah preemyehreet'
Where's the fitting room?	**Где примерочная?**	gdyeh preemyehrahch'-nahyah
Is there a mirror?	**Есть ли у вас зеркало?**	yehst' lyee oo vahss zyehr-kahlah
Does it fit?	**Хорошо сидит?**	khahrahsho seedyeet

FOR NUMBERS, see page 175

It fits very well.	Очень хорошо сидит.	ochyeen' khahrahsho seedyeet
It doesn't fit.	Совсем не годится.	sahvsyehm nyee gah-dyeetsah
It's too ...	Слишком...	slyeeshkahm
short/long tight/loose	коротко/длинно тесно/просторно	korahtkah/dlyeennah tyehsnah/prahstornah
How long will it take to alter?	Сколько времени займёт подгонка?	skol'kah vryehmeenyee zighmyot pahdgonkah

SHOPPING GUIDE

Shoes

I'd like a pair of ...	Дайте мне, пожалуй-ста, пару...	dightyee mnyeh pahzhah-loostah pahroo
shoes/sandals/ boots	туфель/сандалий/ сапог	toofyehl'/sahndahlyeey/ sahpog
These are too ...	Эти слишком...	ehtyee slyeeshkahm
narrow/wide large/small	узкие/широкие большие/маленькие	oozkeeyeh/sheerokeeyeh bahl'shiyeh/mahlyeen'-keeyeh
Do you have a larger size?	Есть ли на номер больше?	yehst' lyee nah nomyeer bol'sheh
I want a smaller size.	Мне нужно на номер меньше.	mnyeh noozhnah nah no-myeer myehn'sheh
Do you have the same in ...?	Есть ли у вас то же самое в...?	yehst' lyee oo vahss to zheh sahmahyeh v
brown/beige	коричневом/бежевом	kahreeshnyeevahm/ byehzhehvahm
black/white	чёрном/белом (тоне)	chyornahm/byehlahm (tonyeh)

Shoes worn out? Here's the key to get them fixed again ...

Can you repair these shoes?	Можно починить эти туфли?	mozhnah pahchyeenyeet' ehtyee tooflyee
I want new soles and heels.	Мне нужны новые подмётки и набойки.	mnyeh noozhni noviyeh pahdmyotkee ee nahboykee
When will they be ready?	Когда будет готово?	kahgdah boodyeht gahto-vah

Clothes and accessories

I'd like a/an/some …	Я хочу купить…	yah khah**chyoo** koo**peet'**
bathing cap	купальную шапочку	koopahl'nooyoo **shah-pahch'koo**
bathing suit	купальный костюм	koopahl'niy kahs**tyoom**
bathing robe	купальный халат	koopahl'niy khah**laht**
bikini	бикини	bee**kee**nyee
blazer	блазер	**blah**zyehr
blouse	блузку	**blooz**koo
boots	сапоги	sahpah**ghee**
bra	лифчик	**lyeef**chyeek
braces (Br.)	подтяжки	pahd**tyahzh**kee
briefs	шорты	**shor**ti
cap	кепку	**kyehp**koo
cape	накидку	nah**keed**koo
cardigan	шерстяной жилет	shirstyee**noy** zhi**lyeht**
coat	пиджак	pyeed**zhahk**
costume	костюм	kahs**tyoom**
dinner jacket	смокинг	**smok**eeng
dress	платье	**plaht'**yeh
dressing gown	халат	khah**laht**
evening dress (woman's)	вечернее платье	vyee**chyehr**nyehyeh **plaht'**yeh
dungarees	рабочие брюки	rah**bo**chyeeyeh **bryoo**kee
frock	платье	**plaht'**yeh
fur coat	меховое пальто	myeekhah**vo**yeh pahl'**to**
fur hat	меховую шапку	myeekhah**voo**yoo **shahp**koo
garters	подвязки	pahd**vyahz**kee
girdle	пояс	**po**yahss
gloves	перчатки	pyeer**chyaht**kee
handkerchief	носовой платок	nahssah**voy** plah**tok**
hat	шляпу	**shlya**hpoo
housecoat	халат	khah**laht**
jacket	куртку	**koort**koo
jeans	джинсы	**dzhin**si
jersey	свитер	**svee**tyehr
jumper (Br.)	джемпер	**dzhehm**pyehr
kerchief	косынку	kahs**sin**koo
knickers	бриджи	**breed**zhi
lingerie	дамское бельё	**dahm**skahyeh byeel'**yo**
necktie	галстук	**gahl**stook
negligé	пеньюар	pyen'**yoo**ahr
nightdress	ночную рубашку	nahch'**noo**yoo roo**bahsh**koo
overcoat	пальто	pahl'**to**
panties	трусики	**troos**seekee

pants (trousers)	брюки	bryookee
panty-girdle	брючный ремень	bryooch'niy reemyehn'
pinafore	передник	pyeeryehdnyeek
pyjamas	пижаму	peezhahmoo
raincoat	дождевик	dahzhdyeevyeek
robe	платье	plaht'yeh
rubber boots	резиновые сапоги	ryeezeenahviyeh sahpah-ghee
sandals	сандалии	sahndahl'yee
scarf	шарф	shahrf
shirt	рубашку	roobahskoo
shoes	туфли	tooflyee
skirt	юбку	yoobkoo
slip	комбинацию	kahmbeenahtsiyoo
slippers	комнатные туфли	komnahtniyeh tooflyee
socks	носки	nahskee
sports jacket	спортивную куртку	spahrtyeevnooyoo koortkoo
stockings	чулки	chyoolkee
stole	меховую накидку	myeekhahvooyoo nahkeedkoo
suit	костюм	kahstyoom
suspenders	подтяжки	pahdtyahzhkee
sweatshirt	спортивный свитер	spahrtyeevniy sveetyehr
swimsuit	купальный костюм	koopahl'niy kahstyoom
tennis shoes	теннисные туфли	tehnyeesniyeh tooflyee
tie	галстук	gahlstook
top coat	пальто	pahl'to
trousers	брюки	bryookee
underpants (men)	кальсоны	kahl'soni
vest (Am.)	жилет	zhilyeht
vest (Br.)	майку	mighkoo
waistcoat	жилет	zhilyeht

belt	пояс	poyahss
buckle	пряжка	pryahzhkah
button	пуговица	poogahveetsah
elastic	резинка	ryeezeenkah
lapel	лацкан	lahtskahn
pocket	карман	kahrmahn
sleeve	рукав	rookahv
zipper	молния	molnyeeyah

Electrical appliances and accessories—Records

While 220 volts AC, 50 cycles, tends to be standard, you'll still find 110–120 volts AC, 50 cycles, in some places. Western plugs are not always the same as Russian ones, but major hotels often have electrical outlets suited to our plugs. If you're planning to undertake extensive travel in the USSR, it's wise to purchase an adapter before leaving for electric appliances you're taking with you. Adapters are hard to find in the Soviet Union.

What's the voltage?	Какое здесь напряжение?	kahkoyyeh zdyehs' nahpryezhehn'yeh
I want a plug for this ...	Дайте мне, пожалуйста, вилку для...	dightyee mnyeh pahzhahloostah vyeelkoo dlyah
Have you a battery for this...?	Есть ли у вас батарейка для...	yehst' lyee oo vahss bahtahryaykah dlyah
This is broken. Can you repair it?	Это не работает. Можно починить?	ehtah nyee rahbotaheet. mozhnah pahchyeenyeet'
When will it be ready?	Когда будет готово?	kahgdah boodyeht gahtovah
I'd like a/an/some ...	Дайте мне, пожалуйста...	dightyee mnyeh pahzhahloostah
adapter	переходную розетку	pyeereekhodnooyoo rahzyehtkoo
amplifier	усилитель	oosseelyeetyehl'
battery	батарейку	bahtahryaykoo
clock	часы	chyeessi
food mixer	миксер	meeksyehr
hair-dryer	сушилку для волос	sooshilkoo dlyah vahloss
iron	утюг	ootyoog
travelling iron	дорожный утюг	dahrozhniy ootyoog
kettle	чайник	chyighnyeek
percolator	кофеварку	kahfyeevahrkoo
plug	вилку	vyeelkoo
radio	приёмник	pryeeyomnyeek
portable radio	портативный приёмник	pahrtahtyeevniy pryeeyomnyeek
razor	электробритву	ehlyehktrahbreetvo
record player	проигрыватель	praheegrivahtyehl'
portable record player	портативный проигрыватель	pahrtahtyeevniy praheegrivahtyehl'

SHOPPING GUIDE

speakers	динамики	dyeenahmyeekyee
tape recorder	магнитофон	mahgnyeetahfon
cassette tape recorder	кассетный магнитофон	kahssyehtniy mahgnyeetahfon
portable tape recorder	портативный магнитофон	pahrtahtyeevniy mahgnyeetahfon
television	телевизор	tyehlyehveezahr
portable television	портативный телевизор	pahrtahtyeevniy tyehlyehveezahr
transformer	трансформатор	trahnsfahrmahtahr

Records

Have you any records by...?	Есть ли у вас пластинки...?	yehst' lyee oo vahss plahstyeenkee
Can I listen to this record?	Можно послушать эту пластинку?	mozhnah pahslooshaht' ehtoo plahstyeenkoo
I'd like a cassette.	Дайте мне кассету.	dightyee mnyeh kahssyehtoo
I want a new needle.	Мне нужна новая игла.	mnyeh noozhnah novahyah eeglah

classical music	классическая музыка	klahsseechyehskahyah moozikah
folk music	народная музыка	nahrodnahyah moozikah
instrumental music	инструментальная музыка	eenstroomyehntahl'nahyah moozikah
jazz	джаз	dzhahz
light music	лёгкая музыка	lyokhkahyah moozikah
orchestral music	оркестровая музыка	ahrkyehstrovahyah moozikah
pop music	«поп»-музыка	pop-moozikah

Hairdresser's—Barber's

In the Soviet Union, women often work as barbers. Men's hair styles vary greatly in the USSR, but shoulder-length hair is still considered a bit foreign.

I don't speak much Russian.	Я плохо говорю по-русски.	yah plokhah gahvahryoo pahrooskee
I want a haircut, please.	Постригите, пожалуйста.	pahstreegheetyee pahzhahloostah
I'd like a shave.	Побрейте, пожалуйста.	pahbryaytyee pahzhahloostah
Cut it short/Leave it fairly long.	Постригите коротко/Оставьте подлиннее.	pahstreegheetyee korahtkah/ahstahvtyee pahdlyeenyehyeh
Scissors only, please.	Только ножницами, пожалуйста.	tol'kah nozhnyeetsahmee pahzhahloostah
A razor-cut, please.	Бритвой, пожалуйста.	breetvigh pahzhahloostah
Don't use the clippers.	Пожалуйста, без ножниц.	pahzhahloostah byehz nozhnyeets
That's enough off.	Так достаточно.	tahk dahstahtahch'nah
A little more off ...	Снимите ещё немножко...	snyeemyeetyee yeeshchyo nyeemnozhkah
the back/neck	на затылке/на шее	nah zahtilkyeh/nah shehveh
the sides/top	по бокам/сверху	pah bahkahm/svyehrkhoo
Don't use any oil, please.	Пожалуйста, ничем не смазывайте.	pahzhahloostah nyeechyehm nyee smahzivightyee
Would you please trim my...?	Пожалуйста, подстригите...	pahzhahloostah pahdstreegheetyee
beard	бороду	borahdoo
moustache	усы	oossi
How much do I owe you?	Сколько я вам должен?	skol'kah yah vahm dolzhehn

FOR TIPPING, see page 1

SHOPPING GUIDE

Ladies' hairdresser's

Can I make an appointment for sometime on Tuesday?	Можно ли условиться на вторник?	mozhnah lyee ooslovitsah nah vtornyeek
I'd like it cut and shaped.	Пожалуйста, постригите и причешите.	pahzhahloostah pahstreegheetyee ee preechyeeshityee

with a fringe	с челкой	s chyolkigh
page-boy style	под мальчика	pahd mahl'chyeekah
a razor cut	бритвой	breetvigh
with ringlets	с локонами	s lokahnahmee
with waves	с завивкой	s zahveevkigh

I want a …	Сделайте мне, пожалуйста,…	zdyehlightyee mnyeh pahzhahloostah
bleach	обесцвечивание	ahbyeestsvyehcheevahn'yeh
colour rinse	оттеночное полоскание	ahttyehnahch'nahyeh pahlahskahn'yeh
dye	окраску	ahkrahskoo
permanent	перманент	pyehrmahnyehnt
tint	окраску	ahkrahskoo
touch up	оттенок	ahttyehnahk
the same colour	тот же самый цвет	tot zheh sahmiy tsvyeht
a darker colour	темнее	tyeemnyehyeh
a lighter colour	светлее	svyeetlyehyeh
auburn/blond/ brunette	каштанового цвета/ под блондинку/ под брюнетку	kahshtahnahvahvah tsvyehtah/pahd blahndyeenkoo/pahd bryoonyehtkoo

Do you have a colour chart?	Есть ли у вас таблица цветов?	yehst' lyee oo vahss tahblyeetsah tsvyeetov
I don't want any hairspray.	Лака не нужно.	lahkah nyee noozhnah
I want a …	Сделайте мне, пожалуйста,…	zdyehlightyee mnyeh pahzhahloostah
manicure/pedicure/ face pack	маникюр/педикюр/ косметическую маску	mahnyeekyoor/pyeedyeekyoor/kahsmyeetyeechyeeskoyoo mahskoo

FOR TIPPING, see page 1

SHOPPING GUIDE

Jeweller's—Watchmaker's

Let's face it: the rate of exchange for rubles makes it hard to find a bargain in the USSR.

Asking

Can you repair this watch?	Вы могли бы починить эти часы?	vi mahglyee bi pahchyeenyeet' ehtyee chyeessi
The ... is broken.	...сломано.	... slomahnah
glass/spring/strap	стекло/пружина/ремешок	styeeklo/proozhinah/ryeemyeeshok
I want this watch cleaned.	Эти часы надо почистить.	ehtyee chyeessi nahdah pahch'eestyeet'
When will it be ready?	Когда они будут готовы?	kahgdah ahnyee boodoot gahtovi
Could I see that, please?	Покажите это, пожалуйста.	pahkahzhityee ehtah pahzhahloostah
I'm just looking around.	Я просто смотрю.	yah prostah smahtryoo
I want a small present.	Мне нужно купить подарок.	mnyeh noozhnah koopeet' pahdahrahk
I don't want anything too expensive.	Ничего слишком дорогого.	nyeechyeevo slyeeshkahm dahrahgovah
I want something...	Я хочу, что-нибудь...	yah khahchyoo shtonyeebood'
better/cheaper/simpler	получше/подешевле/попроще	pahloochsheh/pahdyeeshehvlyeh/pahproshchyeh
Is this real silver?	Это настоящее серебро?	ehtah nahstahyahshchyehyeh syeeryeebro
Have you anything in gold?	Есть ли у вас золотые вещи?	yehst' lyee oo vahss zahlahtiyeh vyehshchyee

If it's made of gold, ask:

How many carats is this?	Сколько здесь каратов?	skol'kah zdyehs' kahrahtahv

When you go to a jeweller's, you've probably got some idea of what you want beforehand. Find out what the article is made of and then look up the Russian name of the article itself in the following lists.

What's it made of?

amber	янтарь	yahntahr'
amethyst	аметист	ahmyeeteeyest
chromium	хром	khrom
copper	медь	myehd'
coral	коралл	kahrahl
crystal	хрусталь	khroostahl'
diamond	бриллиант	bryeel'yahnt
ebony	чёрное дерево	chyornahyeh dyehryeevah
emerald	изумруд	eezoomrood
enamel	эмаль	ehmahl'
glass	стекло	styeeklo
gold	золото	zolahtah
gold plate	позолота	pahzahlotah
ivory	слоновая кость	slahnovayah kost'
jade	гагат	gahgaht
onyx	оникс	ahnyeeks
pearl	жемчуг	zhehmchyoog
platinum	платина	plahtyeenah
ruby	рубин	roobyeen
sapphire	сапфир	sahpfeer
silver	серебро	syeeryeebro
stainless steel	нержавеющая сталь	nyeerzhahvyehyoo-shchyahyah stahl'
topaz	топаз	tahpahz
turquoise	бирюза	beeryoozah

What is it?

I'd like a/an/some…	Я хотел бы купить…	yah khahtyehl bi koopeet'
bangle	браслет	brahslyeht
beads	бусы	boossi
bracelet	браслет	brahslyeht
brooch	брошь	brosh
chain	цепочку	tsehpoch'koo
charm	брелок	bryehlok

cigarette case	портсигар	pahrtsigahr
cigarette lighter	зажигалку	zazhighalkoo
clip	клипс	klyeeps
clock	настольные часы	nahstol'niyeh chyeessi
alarm clock	будильник	boodyeel'nyeek
collar stud	запонку	zahpahnkoo
cross	крестик	kryehstyeek
cuff-links	запонки для манжет	zahpahnkee dlyah mahn-zheht
cutlery	ложки, вилки, ножи	lozhkee veelkee nahzhi
earrings	серьги	syehr'ghee
icon	икону	eekonoo
jewel box	футляр	footlyahr
necklace	ожерелье	ahzhiryehl'yeh
pendant	кулон	koolon
pin	булавку	boolahvkoo
powder compact	пудреницу	poodryehnyeetsoo
ring	кольцо	kahl'tso
engagement ring	обручальное кольцо	ahbroochyahl'nahyeh kahl'tso
signet ring	кольцо с печаткой	kahl'tso s pyeechyahtkigh
wedding ring	обручальное кольцо	ahbroochyahl'nahyeh kahl'tso
silverware	столовое серебро	stahlovahyeh syeeryeebro
snuff box	табакерку	tahbahkyehrkoo
strap	ремешок	ryehmyehshok
chain strap	цепочку	tsehpoch'chkoo
leather strap	кожаный ремешок	kozhahniy ryehmyehshok
watch strap	ремешок для часов	ryehmyehshok dlyah chyeessov
tie-pin	булавку для галстука	boolahvkoo dlyah gahlstookah
vanity case	сумочку	soomahch'koo
watch	часы	chyeessi
pocket watch	карманные часы	kahrmahnniyeh chyeehssi
with a second-hand	с секундной стрелкой	s syeekoondnigh stryehlkigh
wrist-watch	наручные часы	nahrooch'niyeh chyeessi

Laundry—Dry cleaning

The floor manager—usually posted next to the lift—will take care of your laundry. If, however, your hotel doesn't have its own laundry and dry cleaning service, ask the service bureau:

Where's the nearest laundry?	Где ближайшая прачечная?	gdyeh blyeezhighshahyah prahchyeeshnahyah
I want these clothes ...	Эти вещи надо...	ehtyee vyehshchye nahdah
cleaned	почистить	pahchyeestyeet'
pressed	отутюжить	ahtootyoozhit'
ironed	погладить	pahglahdyeet'
washed	выстирать	vistyeeraht'
When will it be ready?	Когда будет готово?	kahgdah boodyeet gah-tovah
I need it ...	Мне нужно...	mnyeh noozhnah
today	сегодня	seevodnyah
tonight	сегодня вечером	seevodnyah vyehchyeerahm
tomorrow	завтра	zahvtrah
before Friday	до пятницы	dah pyahtnyeetsi
Can you ... this?	Можно ли это...?	mozhnah lyee ehtah
mend/patch/ stitch	заштопать/залатать/ зашить	zahshtopaht'/zahlahtaht'/ zahshit'
Can you sew on this button?	Пришейте, пожалуйста, пуговицу.	preeshaytee pahzhah-loostah poogahveetsoo
Can you get this stain out?	Можно вывести это пятно?	mozhnah vivyehstyee ehtah pyahtno
Can this be invisibly mended?	Можно сделать косметическую штопку?	moozhnah zdyehlaht' kahsmyehtyeechyehskoo-yoo stopkoo
This isn't mine.	Это не моё.	ehtah nyee mahyo
There's a hole in this.	Тут дырка.	toot dirkah
Where's my laundry? You promised it for today.	Где моё бельё? Вы мне обещали, что будет готово сегодня.	gdyeh mahyo byeelyo? vi mnyeh ahbyeeshchyahlyee shto boodyeet gahtovah seevodnyah

Photography—Cameras

To be certain, take plenty of film from home. What you are accustomed to may not be available in the Soviet Union. You should be careful about photographing anything of a military nature, as well as airports and harbours. While there is nothing to prevent you from shooting street scenes, it's always best to ask people if they mind being photographed.

Is it all right if I take a picture?	Вы не против, если я вас сниму?	vi nyee **pro**tyeev **yehs**lyee yah vahss snyee**moo**
I'd like a film for this camera.		**digh**tyee mnyeh pahzhah-loostah **plyon**koo dlyah ehtahvah ahpah**rah**tah
	этого аппарата.	
120	шесть на шесть (6 × 6)	shehst' nah shehst'
127	четыре на четыре (4 × 4)	chyeeti**ryeh** nah chyeeti-ryeh
35 mm/ 135	двадцать четыре на тридцать шесть (24 × 36)	**dvah**tsaht' chyeeti**ryeh** nah **tree**tsaht' shehst'
8 mm	восемь миллиметров	**vo**syeem' meel**yee**myeh-trahv
super 8	супер восемь	**soo**pyehr **vo**syeem'
16 mm	шестнадцать милли-метров	shis**naht**saht' meel**yee**-myehtrahv
20/36 exposures	двадцать/тридцать шесть фотографий	**dvah**tsaht'/**tree**tsaht' shehst' fahtah**grah**feey
this size	этого размера	**eh**tahvah rahz**myeh**rah
this ASA/DIN number	это число аса/дин	**eh**tah chyee**slo** ah**ssah**/dyeen
black and white	чёрно-белая	**chyor**nah-**byeh**lahyah
colour negative	цветная негативная	tsvyeht**nah**yah nyehgah-**tyeev**nahyah
colour slide	цветная позитивная	tsvyeht**nah**yah pahzyee-**tyeev**nahyah
artificial light type (indoor)	для искуственного света	dlyah eee**skoost**vyeennah-vah **svyeh**tah
daylight type (outdoor)	для дневного света	dlyah dnyeh**v**novah **svyeh**tah

FOR NUMBERS, see page 175

SHOPPING GUIDE

Processing

How much do you charge for developing?	Сколько стоит проявить плёнку?	skol'kah stooeet prahyah-veet' plyonkoo
I want ... prints of each negative.	Я хочу по... отпечатков от каждого негатива.	yah khahchyoo pah ... ahtpyeechyahtkahv aht kahzhdahvah nyegahtyee-vah
Will you enlarge this, please?	Нельзя ли увеличить?	nyeel'zyah lyee oovyeelyeechyeet'

Accessories

I want a/an/some ...	Я хотел бы купить...	yah khahtyehl bi koopeet'
cable release	тросик	trossyeek
exposure meter	экспонометр	ehkspahnomyehtr
flash bulbs	лампы для вспышки	lahmpi dlyah vspishkee
for black and white	для чёрно-белой плёнки	dlyah chyornah byehligh plyonkyee
for colour	для цветной плёнки	dlyah tsvyehtnoy plyonkyee
filter	фильтр	feel'tr
red/yellow	красный/жёлтый	krashniy/zholtiy
ultra violet	ультрафиолетовый	ool'trahfeeahlyehtahviy
lens	объектив	ahb'yehktyeev
lens cap	крышку объектива	krishkoo ahb'yehktyeevah
tripod	треножник	tryehnozhnyeek

Broken

This camera doesn't work. Can you repair it?	Аппарат не работает. Вы можете исправить?	ahpahraht nyee rahbota-heet. vi mozhehtyee eesprahvyeet'
The film is jammed.	Плёнку заело.	plyonkoo zahyehlah
There's something wrong with the ...	Что-то не в порядке с...	shtotah nyee v pahryahd-kyeh s
exposure counter	установкой выдержки	oostahnovkigh vidyehrzh-kee
film winder	заводом/перемоткой	zahvodahm/pyeereemotkigh
light meter	экспозиметром	ehkspozeemehtrahm
shutter	затвором	zahtvorahm

Provisions

Here's a list of basic food and drink that you might want on a picnic or for the occasional meal in your room.

I'd like a/an/some …, please.	Дайте мне, пожалуйста, …	dightyee mnyeh pahzhahloostah
apples	яблоки	yahblahkee
bananas	бананы	bahnahni
biscuits (cookies)	печенье	pyeechyehn'yeh
bread	хлеб	khlyehb
butter	масло	mahslah
caviar	икру	eekroo
cheese	сыр	syr
chocolate	шоколад	shikahlahd
coffee	кофе	kofyeh
cold meat	холодное мясо	khahlodnahyeh myahssah
cooking fat	жир	zhir
cottage cheese	творог	tvahrog
crackers	крэкер	krehkyehr
crisps (potato chips)	хрустящий картофель	khroostyahshchyeey kahrtofyehl'
cucumbers	огурцы	ahgoortsi
dried figs	сушёный инжир	sooshoniy eenzhir
ham	ветчину	vyeechyeenoo
hamburgers	котлеты	kahtlyehti
ice-cream	мороженое	mahrozhehnahyeh
lemonade	лимонад	lyeemahnahd
lemons	лимоны	lyeemoni
liver sausage	ливерную колбасу	lyeevyehrnooyoo kahlbahssoo
luncheon meat	варёную колбасу	vahryonooyoo kahlbahssoo
macaroni	макароны	mahkahroni
milk	молоко	mahlahko
mustard	горчицу	gahrchyeetsoo
orange squash (drink)	апельсиновый сок	ahpyeel'seenahviy sok
oranges	апельсины	ahpyeel'seeni
pâté	паштет	pahshtyeht
pepper	перец	pyehryehts
pickles	маринованые огурцы	mahreenovahniyeh ahgoortsi
pork	свинину	sveenyeenoo
potatoes	картошку	kahrtoshkoo
raisins	изюм	eezyoom
rolls	булочки	boolah'chkee

salad	салат	sahlaht
sandwiches	бутерброды	bootyeerbrodi
sausages	сосиски	sahsseeskee
sugar	сахар	sahkhahr
sweets (candy)	конфеты	kahnfyehti
tea	чай	chyigh
tomatoes	помидоры	pahmeedori
yoghurt	простоквашу	prahstahkvahshoo

And don't forget …

a bottle opener	открывалку для бутылок	ahtkrivahlkoo dlyah bootilahk
a corkscrew	штопор	shtopahr
matches	спички	speech'kee
(paper) napkins	(бумажные) салфетки	(boomahzhniyeh) sahlfyehtkee
a tin (can) opener	консервный нож	kahnsyehrvniy nozh

Weights and measures

1 kilogram or kilo (kg) = 1000 grams (g)

| 100 g = 3.5 oz. | ½ kg = 1.1 lb. |
| 200 g = 7.0 oz. | 1 kg = 2.2 lb. |

1 oz. = 28.35 g
1 lb. = 453.60 g

---

1 litre (l) = 0.88 imp. quarts = 1.06 U.S. quarts

| 1 imp. quart = 1.14 l | 1 U.S. quart = 0.95 l |
| 1 imp. gallon = 4.55 l | 1 U.S. gallon = 3.8 l |

---

box	коробка	kahrobkah
can	(консервная) банка	(kahnsyehrvnahyah) bahnkah
carton	картонка	kahrtonkah
crate	корзина	kahrzeenah
jar	банка	bahnkah
packet	пакет	pahkyeht
tin	(консервная) банка	(kahnsyehrvnahyah) bahnkah
tube	тюбик	tyoobeek

Souvenirs

When buying antiques, travellers should bear in mind that pre-1917 art objects are generally considered national treasures and may not be taken out of the country. Thus, you can only export antique paintings, sculpture and icons after securing permission from the Ministry of Culture and upon payment of customs duties.

You'll find a whole range of carved and painted birchwood items, Georgian horn goblets and embroidered silk caps at the Beriozka stores where all purchases must be made in foreign currency.

Here are some ideas for souvenir shopping:

abacuses	счёты	shchyoti
amber	янтарь	yahntahr'
chess sets	шахматы	shahkhmahti
fur hats	меховые шапки	myeekhahviyeh shahpkee
icons	иконы	eekoni
lace	кружево	kroozhivah
leather goods	изделия из кожи	eezdyehl'yah eez kozhi
posters	плакаты	plahkahti
rugs from Tekin	текинские ковры	tyehkeenskeeyeh kahvri
Russian cigarettes	папиросы	pahpeerossi
stamps	марки	mahrkee
vodka	водка	vodkah
wooden dolls	матрёшки	mahtryoshkee

Tobacconist's

Many Russians still smoke папиросы (pahpee**ro**ssi) which are almost twice as thick as normal cigarettes but which are half empty. These cigarettes are usually strong, very strong. *Belomore* is a popular brand. Milder ones in modern, Western-looking packs are also available. If you want to try Russian-made cigarettes, ask for a pack of *Stolitchniyeh* or *Yava*. Real Western cigarettes can only be found in hard-currency shops.

Give me a/some..., please.	Дайте мне, пожалуйста, ...	**digh**tyee mnyeh pah**zhah**-loostah
box of ...	коробку ...	kah**rob**koo
cigar	сигару	see**gah**roo
cigarette case	портсигар	pahrtsi**gahr**
cigarette holder	мундштук	moond**shtook**
cigarette lighter	зажигалку	zahzhi**gahl**koo
flints	кремни	kryeh**mn**nyee
lighter	зажигалку	zahzhi**gahl**koo
matches	спички	**speech**'kee
packet ...	пачку ...	**pahch**'koo
packet of cigarettes	пачку сигарет	**pahch**'koo seegah**ryeht**
pipe	трубку	**troob**koo
pipe tobacco	трубочный табак	**troobahch**'niy tah**bahk**
tobacco pouch	кисет	kee**ssyeht**
wick	фитиль	fee**tyeel**'
Have you any ..?	Есть ли у вас ...?	yehst' lyee oo vahss
American cigarettes	американские сигареты	ahmyeeree**kahn**skeeyeh seegah**ryeh**ti
English cigarettes	английские сигареты	ahn**glee**yskeeyeh seegah**ryeh**ti
menthol cigarettes	сигареты с ментолом	seegah**ryeh**ti s myehn**to**lahm
I'd like a carton.	Я возьму блок.	yah vahz'**moo** blok

filter-tipped	с фильтром	s **feel**'trahm
without filter	без фильтра	byehz **feel**'trah

While we're on the subject of cigarettes, suppose you want to offer somebody one?

Would you like a cigarette?	**Не хотите ли сигарету?**	nyee khah**tyee**tyee lyee seegah**ryeh**too
Have one of mine.	**Пожалуйста, мои.**	pah**zhah**loostah mahee
Try one of these.	**Попробуйте мои.**	pah**proboo**ytyee mahee
They're very mild.	**Они очень слабые.**	ah**nyee** ochyeen' **slahb**iyeh
They're a bit strong.	**Они крепкие.**	ah**nyee kryehp**keeyeh

And if somebody offers you one?

Thank you.	**Спасибо.**	spah**ssee**bah
No, thanks.	**Нет, спасибо.**	nyeht spah**ssee**bah
I don't smoke.	**Я не курю.**	yah nyee koor**yoo**
I've given it up.	**Я бросил курить.**	yah **bros**seel koo**reet'**

Your money: banks—currency

As we've already mentioned, you must declare all foreign currency at the customs. Hang on to that declaration since you'll be asked for it when departing. The declaration is required to change rubles back into Western currency and to take your money back out of the Soviet Union.

To change traveller's cheques or foreign currency into rubles, go no farther than the currency-exchange desk in your hotel. Hours vary from place to place, but currency-exchange desks are open considerably longer and are easier to deal with than banks. Remember to carry your passport and currency-control certificate when changing money.

Major credit cards are accepted by most Intourist shops and hotels, but otherwise no Soviet establishments recognize them. Foreign-currency shops also accept most traveller's cheques as do exchange offices.

Banking hours

Monday through Friday from 9.30 a.m. to 12.30 p.m. The airport currency-exchange offices are usually open outside normal hours.

Monetary unit

The monetary system is based on the ruble which is divided into 100 kopecks. Three rubles and 15 kopecks would be abbreviated 3 p. 15 k.

There are coins of 1, 2, 3, 5, 10, 15, 20, 50 kopecks and 1 ruble, and banknotes of 1, 3, 5, 10, 25, 50 and 100 rubles.

Before going

| Where's the nearest bank/currency-exchange office? | Где ближайший банк/обмен денег? | gdyeh blyee**zhigh**shiy bahnk ahb**myehn** dyeh**nyehg** |
| Where can I cash a traveller's cheque (check)? | Где можно разменять дорожные чеки? | gdyeh **mozhna** rahzmyee-**nyaht'** dahro**zhniye chyeh**kee |

Inside

I want to change some dollars.	Мне нужно обменять доллары.	mnyeh **noozh**nah ahb-myee**nyaht' dolah**ri
I'd like to change some pounds.	Мне нужно обменять фунты.	mnyeh **noozh**nah ahb-myee**nyaht' foon**ti
Here's my passport.	Вот мой паспорт.	vot moy **pahs**pahrt
What's the exchange rate?	Какой валютный курс?	kah**koy** vah**lyoot**niy koors
What rate of commission do you charge?	Сколько вы берёте за обмен?	**skol'**kah vi byee**ryotyee** zah ahb**myehn**
I have ...	У меня ...	oo myee**nyah**
an introduction from ... a credit card	рекомендательное письмо ... кредитная карточка	ryeh**kahm**yehn**dahtyehl'**-nahyeh pees'**mo** kryeh**dyeet**nahyah **kahr**tahch'kah
I'm expecting some money from ... Has it arrived yet?	Для меня должны быть деньги из ... Они уже пришли?	dlyah myee**nyah** dah**lzhni** bit' **dyehn'**ghee eez ... ah**nyee** oo**zheh** preesh**lyee**
Give me ... 50-ruble notes (bills) and some small change, please.	Дайте мне, пожалуйста, ... пятидесяти-рублёвок, остальное мелочью.	**digh**tyee mnyeh pah**zhah**-loostah ... pyee**tyeedyee**-ssyee**tyeer**roo**blyo**vahk ahstahl'**noyeh myeh**lah-ch'yoo
Give me ... large notes and the rest in small notes.	Дайте мне пожалуйста ... крупных купюр, а остальное мелкими купюрами.	**digh**tyee mnyeh pah**zhah**-loostah ... **kroop**nikh koo**pyoor** ah ahstahl'**noyeh myehl**keemee koo**pyoo**-rahmee

FOR NUMBERS, see page 175

BANK

| Could you check that again, please? | **Проверьте ещё раз, пожалуйста?** | prahvyehrtyee yeeshchyo rahz pahzhahloostah |
| Where should I sign? | **Где подписаться?** | gdyeh pahdpeessahtsah |

Currency converter

In a world of fluctuating currencies, we can offer no more than this do-it-yourself chart. You can get information about exchange rates from banks, travel agents and tourist offices. Why not fill in this chart, too, for handy reference?

USSR	£	$
10 kopecks		
50 kopecks		
1 ruble		
5 rubles		
25 rubles		
50 rubles		
100 rubles		

BANK

At the post office

Post offices can be identified by the word почта (**poch**'tah). Mail boxes are painted blue. Hours are generally from 9 a.m. to 6 or 7 p.m. Major hotels have their own branches of the post office for postal, telegraph, telex and telephone services. Don't forget that international postal money orders can only be cashed at banks.

Where's the nearest post-office?	Где ближайшая почта?	gdyeh blyee**zhigh**shahyah **poch**'tah
What time does the post-office open/ close?	В котором часу от- крывается/закры- вается почта?	v kah**to**rahm chyee**ssoo** ahtkri**vah**eetsah/zahkri- **vah**eetsah **poch**'tah
What window do I go to for stamps?	В каком окне про- дают марки?	v kah**kom** ahk**nyeh** prahdah**yoot** **mah**rkee
I want some stamps, please.	Дайте мне, пожа- луйста, марки.	**digh**tye mnyeh pah**zhah**- loostah **mah**rkee
I want ... 4-kopeck stamps and ... 6-kopeck ones.	Я хочу ... марок по 4 копейки и ... марки по 6 копеек.	yah khah**chyoo** ... **mah**rahk pah 4 kah**pyay**kee ee ... **mah**rkee pah 6 kah**pyeh**yehk
What's the postage for a letter to the United States?	Сколько стоит пись- мо в Соединенные Штаты?	**skol**'kah **sto**eet pees'mo v sahyehdyee**nyon**niyeh **shtah**ti
What's the postage for a postcard to Great Britain?	Сколько стоит от- крытка в Англию?	**skol**'kah **sto**eet ahk**krit**kah v **ahn**glyeeyoo
When will this letter get there?	Когда придёт это письмо?	kah**gdah** pree**dyot** **eh**tah pees'mo
Do all letters go airmail?	Авиапочтой идут все письма?	ahveeah**poch**'tigh ee**doot** vsyeh **pees**'mah
Do I need to fill in a customs decla- ration?	Нужно ли заполнить таможенную декла- рацию?	**noozh**nah lyee zah**pol**nyeet' tah**mo**zhehnooyoo dyeh- klah**rah**tsiyoo
I want to register this letter.	Я хочу послать это письмо заказным.	yah khah**chyoo** pah**slaht**' **eh**tah pees'mo zahkah**znim**

Where's the letter-box?	Где почтовый ящик?	gdyeh pahch'**to**viy **yah**-shchyeek
I want to send this by…	Пожалуйста…	pah**zhah**loostah
air mail	авиапочтой	ahveeah**poch'**tigh
express (special delivery)	с нарочным	s **nah**rahch'nim
recorded delivery	с уведомлением о вручении	s oovyehdahm**lyehn**'yehm ah vroo**chyehn**'yee
registered mail	заказным	zahkah**znim**
Where is the poste restante (general delivery)?	Где окно до востребования?	gdyeh ah**kno** dah vahs-**tryehb**bahvahn'yah
Is there any mail for me? My name is…	Нет ли для меня писем? Меня зовут…	nyeht lyee dlyah myee**nyah** **pee**ssyehm? myee**nyah** zah**voot**
Here's my passport.	Вот мой паспорт.	vot moy **pahs**pahrt

| ПОЧТОВЫЕ МАРКИ | STAMPS |
| ПОСЫЛКИ | PARCELS |

Telegrams

Telegrams must be paid for on the spot; you can't reverse the charges.

Where's the (nearest) telegraph office?	Где (ближайший) телеграф?	gdyeh (blyee**zhigh**shiy) tyehl**yeh**grahf
I want to send a telegram. May I have a form, please?	Я хочу послать телеграмму. Пожалуйста, бланк.	yah khah**chyoo** pah**slaht'** tyehl**yeh**grahmoo. pah**zhah**loostah blahnk
How much is it per word?	Сколько нужно платить за слово?	**skol**'kah **noo**zhnah plah**tyeet'** zah **slo**vah
How long will a telegram to Boston take?	Сколько времени идёт телеграмма в Бостон?	**skol**'kah **vryeh**myeenyee ee**dyot** tyehl**yeh**grahmah v **bos**ton

Telephoning

When phoning from a public telephone booth, deposit the coin *before* picking up the receiver. Long-distance calls may be made from hotel rooms or, in major centres, by going to the telephone and telegraph office. International calls are best placed through the hotel service desk, and if you are in a position to do so, well in advance. If not, arm yourself with patience; a two-hour wait is perfectly usual. Telex messages can also be handled by hotels and telephone offices.

General

Where's the telephone?	Где телефон?	gdyeh tyehlyeh**fon**
Where's the nearest telephone booth?	Где ближайшая телефонная будка?	· gdyeh blyee**zhigh**shahyah tyehlyeh**fonn**ahyah **bood**kah
May I use your phone?	Можно от вас позвонить?	**mozh**nah aht vahss pahzvah**nyeet'**
Have you a telephone directory?	Нет ли у вас телефонной книги?	nyeht lyee oo vahss tyehlyeh**fonn**igh **knyee**ghee
Can you help me get this number?	Помогите мне, пожалуйста, найти этот номер?	pahmah**ghee**tyee mnyeh pah**zhah**loostah nigh**tyee** **eh**taht **no**myeer

Operator

Do you speak English?	Вы говорите по-английски?	vi gahvah**ree**tyee pahahng**lyee**yskee
Good morning. I want 12-34-56.	Доброе утро. Дайте мне номер 12-34-56.	**do**brahyeh **oo**trah. **dight**yee mnyeh **no**myeer 12-34-56
Can I dial direct?	Я могу сам набрать?	yah mah**goo** sahm nah**braht'**
Will you tell me the cost of the call afterwards?	Сообщите мне потом, пожалуйста, сколько будет стоить разговор.	sahb**shchyee**tyee mnyeh pah**tom** pah**zhah**loostah **skol**'kah **bood**yeet **sto**eet' rahzgah**vor**

FOR NUMBERS, see page 175

TELEPHONE

Speaking

I want to speak to …	Позовите, пожалуйста…,	pahzah**vyee**tyee pahzhah-loostah
Would you put me through to …?	Пожалуйста, соедините меня с…	pahzhahloostah sahyee-dyee**nyee**tyee myee**nyah** s
I want extension …	Добавочный…	dah**bah**vahch'niy
Is that …?	Это…?	**eh**tah
Hello. This is …	Алло! Говорит…	ah**llo**! gahvah**reet**

Bad luck

Would you try again later, please?	Пожалуйста, попробуйте еще раз попозже.	pahzhahloostah pah**pro**-booytyee yee**shchvo** rahz pah**pozh**zheh
Operator, you gave me the wrong number.	Вы мне дали не тот номер.	vi mnyeh **dah**lyee nyee tot **no**myeer

In case you have to spell your name or take down the incomprehensible name of a street, here's how the letters of the Russian alphabet are pronounced:

а	ah		р	ehr
б	beh		с	ehs
в	veh		т	teh
г	geh		у	oo
д	deh		ф	ehf
е	yeh		х	khah
ё	yoh		ц	tseh
ж	zheh		ч	chyah
з	zeh		ш	shah
и	ee		щ	shchyah
й	ee **kraht**kahyeh		ъ	tv'**yor**diy znahk
к	kah		ы	i
л	ehl		ь	m'**yahkh**koy znahk
м	ehm		э	eh
н	ehn		ю	yoo
о	o		я	yah
п	peh			

Not there

When will she be back?	**Когда она вернётся?**	kahg**dah** ahnah vyeer**nyo**tsah
Will you tell her I called? My name's...	**Передайте ей, пожалуйста, что звонил...**	pyeeree**dight**yee yay pah**zhah**loostah shto zvah**nyeel**
Would you ask her to call me?	**Попросите её, по-жалуйста, позвонить мне.**	pahprah**ssee**tyee yee**yo** pah**zhah**loostah pahzvah**nyeet'** mnyeh
Would you take a message, please?	**Нельзя ли передать-ей несколько слов?**	nyeel'**zyah** lyee pyeeree**daht'** yay **nyehs**kahl'kah slov

Charges

What was the cost of that call?	**Сколько стоил разговор?**	skol'kah **sto**eel rahzgah**vor**
I want to pay for the call.	**Я хочу заплатить за разговор.**	yah khah**chyoo** zahplah**tyeet'** zah rahzgah**vor**

Вас вызывают по телефону.	There's a telephone call for you.
Вас просят к телефону.	You're wanted on the telephone.
Какой номер вам нужен?	What number are you calling?
Телефон занят.	The line's engaged (busy).
Не отвечают.	There's no answer.
У вас неправильный номер.	You've got the wrong number.
Телефон не работает.	The phone is out of order.
Его сейчас нет.	He's out at the moment.

TELEPHONE

The car

Filling station

Petrol is sold in units of 10 litres and is paid for with coupons, which can be bought from Intourist. High-grade and diesel are sometimes difficult to find. Service stations are nearly all self-service: you pay first and then fill up.

Where's the nearest filling station?	Где ближайшая заправочная станция?	gdyeh blyee**zhigh**shahyah zah**prah**vahch'nahyah **stah**ntsiyah
I want... litres, please.	Дайте мне, пожа-луйста, ... литров.	**digh**tyee mnyeh pah**zhah**-loostah... **lyee**trahv
ten/twenty/fifty	десять/двадцать/пятьдесят	**dyeh**ssyaht/**dvah**tsaht/peedyee**ssyaht**
I want ... litres of standard/premium.	Дайте мне ... литров обыкновенного/высшего качества.	**digh**tyee mnyeh ... **lyee**trahv ahbiknah**vyehn**-nahvah/**vish**shehvah **kah**chyehstvah
Give me 50 rubles' worth of ...	Дайте мне, пожа-луйста ... на 50 рублей.	**digh**tyee mnyeh pah**zhah**-loostah... nah 50 roob**lyah**
Fill it up, please.	Полный бак, пожа-луйста.	**pol**niy bahk pah**zhah**-loostah

Fluid measures					
litres	imp. gal.	U.S. gal.	litres	imp. gal.	U.S. gal.
5	1.1	1.3	30	6.6	7.8
10	2.2	2.6	35	7.7	9.1
15	3.3	3.9	40	8.8	10.4
20	4.4	5.2	45	9.9	11.7
25	5.5	6.5	50	11.0	13.0

Check the oil and water, please.	Проверьте, пожалуйста, масло и воду.	prahvyehrtyee pahzhahloostah **mahs**lah ee **vo**doo
Give me … litres of oil.	Дайте мне, пожалуйста, … литров масла.	**digh**tyee mnyeh pahzhahloostah … **lyee**trahv **mahs**lah
Top (fill) up the battery with distilled water.	Долейте дистиллированной воды в аккумулятор.	dah**lyay**tyee dyeestyee**lyee**rahvahnigh vah**di** v ahkoomoo**lyah**tahr

Tire pressure			
lb./sq. in.	kg/cm²	lb./sq. in.	kg/cm²
10	0.7	26	1.8
12	0.8	27	1.9
15	1.1	28	2.0
18	1.3	30	2.1
20	1.4	33	2.3
21	1.5	36	2.5
23	1.6	38	2.7
24	1.7	40	2.8

Would you check the tires?	Проверьте, пожалуйста, давление в шинах.	prahvehrtyee pahzhahloostah dah**vlyehn**'yeh v **shi**nahkh
The pressure should be 1.6 front, 1.8 rear.	Давление должно быть 1,6 впереди и 1,8 сзади.	dah**vlyehn**'yeh dahlzhno bit' 1,6 vpyeeryeed**yee** ee 1,8 **szah**dyee
Check the spare tire, too, please.	Проверьте, пожалуйста, и запасное колесо.	prahvehrtyee pahzhahloostah ee zahpahs**no**yeh kahlyee**sso**
Can you mend this puncture (fix this flat)?	Можно заделать этот прокол?	**mozh**nah zah**dyeh**laht' ehtaht prah**kol**
Will you change this tire, please?	Поставьте, пожалуйста, новую покрышку.	pah**stahv**tyee pahzhahloostah **no**vooyoo pah**krish**koo

Would you clean the windscreen (windshield)?	Помойте, пожалуйста, переднее стекло.	pahmoytyee pahzhahloostah pyeeryehdnyeeyeh styeeklo
Have you a road map of this district?	Есть ли у вас карта дорог этого района?	yehst' lyee oo vahss kahrtah dahrog ehtahvah righonah
Where are the toilets?	Где туалет?	gdyeh tooahlyeht

Asking the way—Street directions

Excuse me.	Простите.	prahstyeetyee
Can you tell me the way to …?	Как проехать к …?	kahk prahyehkhaht' k
How do I get to …?	Как доехать до …?	kahk dahyehkhaht dah
Where does this road lead to?	Куда идёт эта дорога?	koodah eedyot ehtah dahrogah
Can you show me on this map where I am?	Покажите мне, пожалуйста, где я нахожусь.	pahkahzhityee mnyeh pahzhahloostah gdyeh yah 'nahkhahzhoos
How far is it to … from here?	Сколько времени ехать отсюда до …?	skol'kah vryehmyeenyee yehkhaht' ahtsyoodah dah

Miles into kilometres									
1 mile = 1.609 kilometres (km)									
miles	10	20	30	40	50	60	70	80	90	100
km	16	32	48	64	80	97	113	129	145	161

Kilometres into miles												
1 kilometre (km) = 0.62 miles												
km	10	20	30	40	50	60	70	80	90	100	110	120	130
miles	6	12	19	25	31	37	44	50	56	62	68	75	81

Это не та дорога.	You're on the wrong road.
Вам нужно ехать прямо.	Go straight ahead.
Это там, левее (правее).	It's down there on the left (right).
Поезжайте по этой дороге.	Go that way.
До первого (второго) перекрёстка.	Go to the first (second) cross-road.
Сверните налево (направо) у светофора.	Turn left (right) at the traffic lights.

In the rest of this section we'll be more closely concerned with the car itself. We've divided it into two parts:

Part A contains general advice on motoring in the USSR. It's essentially for reference and is therefore to be browsed over, preferably in advance.

Part B is concerned with the practical details of accidents and breakdown. It includes a list of car parts and a list of things that may go wrong with them. All you have to do is to show it to the garage mechanic and get him to point to the items required.

Part A

Customs—Documentation

You'll require the following documents:

  passport with visa
  driving licence (either international or Russian translation of
    home licence)
  ownership and registration papers
  Intourist voucher as a proof of payment for your journey

Licence plates and nationality sticker must be on the car. Insurance coverage is on a voluntary basis. You may take out insurance with the Soviet State Insurance Company *(Ingosstrakh)* by going through Intourist.

You've got to set up your itinerary before making a car trip in the USSR. Along with camping coupons, you'll also be using Intourist petrol tickets.

Here's my ...	Вот...	vot
driving licence	мои права	mahee prahvah
passport	мой паспорт	moy pahspahrt
visa	моя виза	mahyah veezah
I want to hire a car.	Я хочу взять напрокат машину.	yah khahchyoo vzyaht' nahprahkaht mahshinoo
I want to take out automobile insurance.	Я хочу застраховать машину.	yah khahchyoo zahstrahkhahvaht' mahshinoo
We're planning to go to Moscow by way of Minsk.	Мы хотим ехать в Москву через Минск.	mi khahtyeem yehkhaht' v mahskvoo chyehryeez meensk
Can you tell me the way to the main road?	Как проехать к магистрали?	kahk prahyehkhaht' k mahgheestrahlyee
How long does it take to get to Leningrad?	Сколько ехать до Ленинграда?	skol'kah yehkhaht' dah lyehnyeengrahdah

CAR—INFORMATION

FOR CAR RENTAL, see page 26

Roads

You may select any one of a dozen routes to see the Soviet Union. Among the most popular itineraries are Brest–Minsk–Moscow (coming into the USSR from Poland) and Julja–Urpala–Leningrad–Moscow (entry at the Finnish border).

You'll certainly be using paved roads, but there's no telling about snow conditions from October to March. It's best to drive at a moderate speed—especially if it's your first time over the road.

Traffic

Traffic regulations are complex in the Soviet Union but similar to the highway code of other countries. Drive on the right, passing on the left where prudent. The speed limit in all cities and towns is 60 kilometres per hour and 90 outside towns—except where signs permitting higher speeds are displayed. Horns may not be sounded in residential areas except to prevent an accident. In urban driving after dark, only parking lights are used.

While the accident rate is held down by the fact that there is relatively little private automobile traffic, driving "under the influence" is just as big a problem in the Soviet Union as it is in any Western country.

Use common sense when parking. Obey parking regulations which will be indicated by signs. A few of these are found on pages 160 and 161.

A few of these are found on pages 160 and 161.

Excuse me. May I park here?	Простите. Можно тут поставить машину?	prahstyeetyee. mozhnah toot pahstahveet' mahshinoo
How long may I park here?	Надолго ли можно тут оставить машину?	nahdolgah lyee mozhnah toot ahstahveet' mahshinoo
What's the charge for parking here?	Сколько это будет стоить?	skol'kah ehtah boodyet stoeet'

CAR—INFORMATION

Russian road signs

Here are some of the main signs and notices you are likely to
encounter when driving in the Soviet Union. Obviously, they
should be studied in advance. You can't drive and read at the
same time!

CAR—INFORMATION

ВЕЛОСИПЕДИСТЫ	cyclists
ВНИМАНИЕ, ВПЕРЕДИ ВЕДУТСЯ РАБОТЫ	roadworks in progress (men working)
(ВНИМАНИЕ) ПЕШЕХОДЫ	(watch out for) pedestrians
ВСТРЕЧНОЕ ДВИЖЕНИЕ	oncoming traffic
ВЪЕЗД ЗАПРЕЩЁН	no entry
ДВИЖЕНИЕ В ОДИН РЯД	traffic in single lane
ДЕРЖИТЕСЬ ПРАВОЙ СТОРОНЫ	keep right
КАМНЕПАД	loose gravel
НЕ ЗАДЕРЖИВАТЬСЯ	no waiting
ОБГОН ЗАПРЕЩЁН	no overtaking (passing)
ОБОЧИНА	soft shoulders
ОБЪЕЗД	diversion (detour)
ОГРАНИЧЕНИЕ СКОРОСТИ	reduce speed
ОДНОСТОРОННЕЕ ДВИЖЕНИЕ	one-way traffic
ОПАСНО	danger
ОПАСНЫЙ ПОВОРОТ	dangerous bend (curve)
ОСТАНОВКА АВТОБУСА	bus stop
ПЛОХАЯ ДОРОГА	bad road surface
СВЕТОФОР ЗА СТО МЕТРОВ	traffic lights at 100 metres
СКВОЗНОГО ПРОЕЗДА НЕТ	no through road (dead-end road)
СТОЯНКА ЗАПРЕЩЕНА	no parking
СУЖЕНИЕ ДОРОГИ	bottleneck

FOR INTERNATIONAL ROAD SIGNS, see p. 160–161

Part B

Accidents

This section is confined to immediate aid. The legal problems of responsibility and settlement can be taken care of at a later stage.

Your first concern will be for the injured.

Is anyone hurt?	**Никто не ранен?**	nyee**kto** nyee **rah**nyeen
Don't move.	**Не двигайтесь.**	nyee **dvee**ghightyeess
It's all right. Don't worry.	**Всё в порядке. Не беспокойтесь.**	vsyo v pah**ryahd**keh. nyee byeespah**koy**tyeess
Where's the nearest telephone?	**Где ближайший телефон?**	gdyeh blyee**zhigh**shiy tyeh-lyeh**fon**
Can I use your telephone? There's been an accident.	**Можно от вас позвонить? Несчастный случай на дороге!**	**mozh**nah aht vahss pahz-vah**nyeet'**? nyee**shchyahs**-niy **sloo**chyigh nah dah**rogh**yeh
Call a doctor (ambulance) quickly.	**Вызовите скорее врача (скорую помощь).**	vizah**vee**tyee skah**ryay** vrah**chyah** (**skoro**oyoo **po**mahshch')
There are people injured.	**Есть раненые.**	yehst' **rah**nyehniyeh
Help me get them out of the car.	**Помогите мне вытащить их из автомобиля.**	pahmah**ghee**tyee mnyeh **vi**tahshchyeet' eekh eez ahvtahmah**bee**lyah

Police—Exchange of information

Please call the police.	**Вызовите, пожалуйста, милицию.**	vizah**vee**tyee pah**zhah**-loostah mee**lyee**tsiyoo
There's been an accident.	**Несчастный случай.**	nyee**shchyahs**niy **sloo**chyigh
It's about ... kilometres from ...	**Примерно в ... километрах от ...**	pree**myeh**rnah v ... keelah**myeh**trahkh aht
I'm on the Brest—Minsk road, ... kilometres from Minsk.	**Я на дороге Брест-Минск, в ... километрах от Минска.**	yah nah dah**rogh**yeh bryehst meensk v ... keelah**myeht**-rahkh aht **mee**nskah

Here's my name and address.	**Вот моё имя и адрес.**	vot mah**yo ee**myah ee **ah**dryehss
Would you mind acting as a witness?	**Вы согласны быть свидетелем?**	vi sah**glahs**ni bit' sveed**yeh**tyehlyehm
I'd like an interpreter.	**Мне нужен пере- водчик.**	mnyeh **noo**zhehn pyeeryee- **vo**dchyeek

Note: You should report the accident to the nearest Intourist office.

Breakdown

... and that's what we'll do with this section: break it down into four phases.

1. *On the road*
   You ask where the nearest garage is.

2. *At the garage*
   You tell the mechanic what is wrong.

3. *Finding the trouble*
   He tells you what he thinks is wrong.

4. *Getting it fixed*
   You tell him to fix it and, once that's over, settle the account (or argue about it).

Phase 1—On the road

Where is the nearest garage?	**Где ближайшая станция обслужи- вания?**	gdyeh blyee**zhigh**shahyah **stahn**tsiyah ahb**sloozh** i- vahn'yah
Excuse me. My car has broken down. May I use your phone?	**У меня остановилась машина. Можно от вас позвонить?**	oo my**ee**nyah ahstahnah- **vee**lahss mah**shi**nah. **mozh**nah aht vahss pa- **zvahn**yeet'
What's the telephone number of the nearest garage?	**Какой телефон ближайшей станции обслуживания?**	kah**koy** tyeh**lyeh**fon blyee- **zhigh**shay **stahn**tsiee ahb**slooz**hivahn'yah
I've had a break- down at...	**У меня остановилась машина в...**	oo my**ee**nyah ahstahnah- **vee**lahss mah**shi**nah v

We're on the Odessa–Kiev road, about 15 kilometres from Kiev.	Мы на шоссе Одесса-Киев, приблизительно в 15 километрах от Киева.	mi nah shahsseh ahdyehssah-keeyehv preeblyeezeetyeel'nah v 15 keelahmyehtrahkh aht keeyehvah
Can you send a mechanic?	Можно прислать механика?	mozhnah preeslaht' myeekhahnyeekah
Can you send a truck to tow my car?	Можно прислать грузовик и взять на буксир мою машину?	mozhnah preeslaht' groozahveek ee vzyaht' nah bookseer mahyoo mahshinoo
How long will you be?	Когда вы приедете?	kahgdah vi preeyehdyeetyee

Phase 2—At the garage

Can you help me?	Вы можете мне помочь?	vi mozhityee mnyeh pahmoch'
Are you the mechanic?	Вы механик?	vi myeekhahnyeek
I don't know what's wrong with it.	Я не знаю, что случилось.	yah nyee znahyoo shto sloochyeelahss
I think there's something wrong with the ...	Я думаю, что ... не в порядке.	yah doomahyoo shto ... nyee v pahryahdkyeh
battery	аккумулятор	ahkoomoolyahtahr
brakes	тормоза	tahrmahzah
bulbs	лампы	lahmpi
clutch	сцепление	stsehplyehn'yeh
cooling system	охлаждение	ahkhlahzhdyehn'yeh
contact	контакт	kahntahkt
dimmers	переключатель переднего освещения	pyeereeklyoochyahtyehl' pyeeryehdnyeevah ahsvyeeshchyehn'yah
dynamo	динамо	dyeenahmah
electrical system	электрооборудование	ehlyehktrahahbahroodahvahn'yeh
engine	мотор	mahtor
gears	передачи	pyeeryeedahchyee
handbrake	ручной тормоз	rooch'noy tormahz
headlight	фары	fahri
horn	гудок	goodok

ignition	зажигание	zahzhigahn'yeh
indicator	указатель поворота	ookahzahtyehl' pahvahro-tah
lights	свет	svyeht
brake lights	тормозные огни	tahrmahzniyeh ahgnyee
rear (tail) lights	хвостовое освещение	khvahstahvoyeh ahsvyeeshchyehn'yeh
lubrication system	система смазки	seestyehmah smahzkee
pedal	педаль	pyeedahl'
reflectors	отражатели	ahtrahzhahtyeelyee
sparking plugs	свечи	svyehchyee
starting motor	стартер	stahrtyehr
steering	рулевое управление	roolyeevoyeh ooprahvlehn'yeh
suspension	подвеска	pahdvyehskah
transmission	коробка передач	kahrobkah pyehryehdahch'
turn signal	указатель поворота	ookahzahtyehl' pahvahro-tah
wheels	колёса	kahlyossah
wipers	стеклоочистители	styehklahahchyeestyee-tyeelyee

RIGHT	LEFT	FRONT	BACK
СПРАВА	**СЛЕВА**	**ПЕРЕДНЯЯ СТОРОНА**	**ЗАДНЯЯ СТОРОНА**
(**sprah**vah)	(**slyeh**vah)	(pyee**ryehd**nahyah stahrah**nah**)	(**zahd**nyahyah stahrah**nah**)

It's …

bad	плохо	plokhah
blowing	утечка	ootyehch'kah
broken	сломалось	slahmahlahss
burnt	сгорело	sgahryehlah
cracked	треснуло	tryehsnoolah
defective	испорчено	eesporchyeenah
disconnected	разъединилось	rahzyehdyeenyeelahss
dry	высохло	vissahkhlah
frozen	замёрзло	zahmyorzlah
jammed	заело	zahyehlah
knocking	стучит	stoochyeet
leaking	течёт	tyeechyot
loose	болтается	bahltaheetsah

misfiring	перебой зажигания	pyeeree**boy** zahzhigahn'yah
noisy	шумит	shoo**meet**
not working	не действует	nyee **dyayst**vooeet
overheating	перегревается	pyeeryeegryeh**vah**eetsah
short-circuiting	замыкает накоротко	zahmikaheet nahkahrahtkah
slack	разболталось	rahzbahl**tah**lahss
slipping	буксует	book**soo**eet
stuck	заело	zah**yeh**lah
vibrating	вибрирует	veebree**roo**eet
weak	слабо	**slah**bah
worn	износилось	eeznahs**syee**lahss
The car won't start.	Мотор не запускается.	mah**tor** nyee zahpooskah-**eet**sah
It's locked and the keys are inside.	Автомобиль заперт, а ключи внутри.	ahvtahmah**beel'** zah-pyehrt ah klyoo**chyee** vnootree
The radiator is leaking.	Радиатор течёт.	rahdyee**ah**tahr tyee**chyot**
The idling needs adjusting.	Нужно отрегулировать холостой ход.	**noozh**nah ahtryehgoolyee-rahvat' khalahs**toy** khod
The clutch engages too quickly.	Сцепление слишком быстрое.	stsiplyehn'yeh **slyeesh**kahm bistrahyeh
The steering wheel's vibrating.	Рулевое колесо вибрирует.	roolyee**voyeh** kahlyee**sso** veebree**rooyeht**
The wipers are smearing.	Стеклоочистители плохо действуют.	styehklahahchyees**tyee**tyee-lyee **plokhah** **dyayst**vooyoot
The pneumatic suspension is weak.	Пневматическая система слаба.	pnyehvmah**tyee**chyehs-kahyah sees**tyeh**mah **slah**bah
The pedal needs adjusting.	Нужно отрегулировать педаль.	**noozh**nah ahtrehgoolyee-rahvat' pyeh**dahl'**

Now that you've explained what's wrong, you'll want to know how long it'll take to repair it and arrange yourself accordingly.

How long will it take to repair?	Сколько времени займёт ремонт?	**skol'**kah **vryeh**myeenyee zigh**myot** ree**mont**
How long will it take to find out what's wrong?	Когда вы будете знать, что не в порядке?	kahg**dah** vi **boo**dyehtyeh znaht' shto nyee v pah**ryahd**keh

Suppose I come back in half an hour (tomorrow)?	**Мне прийти через полчаса (завтра)?**	mnyeh preeytyee chyehreez polchyeessah (zahvtrah)
Is there a place to stay nearby?	**Есть ли поблизости гостиница?**	yehst' lyee pahblyeezah-styee gahstyeenyeetsah
May I use your phone?	**Можно от вас позвонить?**	mozhnah aht vahss pahzvahnyeet'

Phase 3—Finding the trouble

If you don't know what's wrong with the car, it's up to the mechanic to find the trouble. You can ask him what has to be repaired by handing him the book and pointing to the Russian text below.

Просмотрите, пожалуйста, этот алфавитный список и ука-жите повреждённую часть. Если ваш клиент захочет уз-нать, что не в порядке, выберите подходящий термин из второго списка (сломан, короткое замыкание и.т.д).*

автоматическая передача	automatic transmission
аккумулятор	battery
аккумуляторная жидкость	battery liquid
аккумуляторные элементы	battery cells
амортизатор	shock absorber
бензиновый насос	fuel pump
блок	block
вал	shaft
валы	stems
вентилятор	fan
водяной насос	water pump
воздушный фильтр	air filter
головка цилиндра	cylinder head

* Please look at the following alphabetical list and point to the defective item. If your customer wants to know what is wrong with it, pick the applicable term from the next list (broken, short-circuited, etc.).

динамо	dynamo (generator)
диск муфты сцепления	clutch plate
запальные свечи	sparking plugs
зубцы	teeth
зубчатая рейка и шестерня	rack and pinion
кабель запальной свечи	sparking plug leads
кабель распределителя зажигания	distributor leads
карбюратор	carburettor
карданный шарнир	universal joint
картер коленчатого вала	crankcase
картер рулевого управления	steering box
катушка зажигания	ignition coil
клапан	valve
коленчатый вал	crankshaft
колеса	wheels
колодки	shoes
колонка руля	steering column
кольца	rings
контакт	contact
коробка передач	transmission
коробка скоростей	gear box
масляный фильтр	oil filter
мембрана	diaphragm
мотор	engine
насос	pump
основной подшипник	main bearings
педаль сцепления	clutch pedal
передача	gear
переключение	connection
пневматическая подвеска	pneumatic suspension
подвеска	suspension
подшипник	bearings
поплавок	float
поршень	piston
поршневые кольца	piston rings
прокладка	lining
прокладка головки цилиндра	cylinder head gasket
пружины амортизатора	pressure springs
радиатор	radiator
распределитель зажигания	distributor
распределительный вал	camshaft
рессоры	springs
рулевое управление	steering
система охлаждения	cooling system
стабилизатор	stabilizer

стартер	starter
сцепление	clutch
термостат	thermostat
топливный фильтр	petrol filter
тормоз	brake
тормозной барабан	brake drum
трос	cable
цилиндр	cylinder
щетки	brushes
электрооборудование	electrical system

В следующем списке находятся слова, объясняющие, что случилось с машиной или что нужно с нею сделать.*

быстрый	quick
вибрирует	vibrating
возобновить	to reline
высокий	high
грязный	dirty
деформированный	warped
зазор	play
заменить	to replace
замерз	frozen
зарядить	to charge
застрял	stuck
затянуть	to tighten
изношен	worn
короткий	short
короткое замыкание	short-circuit
низкий	low
ослаб	loose
ослабить	to loosen
отрегулировать	to adjust

---

* The following list contains words about what is wrong or what may need to be
done with the car.

перебой зажигания	misfiring	
перегревается	overheating	
поврежден	defective	
почистить	to clean	
притереть	to grind in	
прокол	puncture	
ржавый	corroded	
сгорел	burnt	
слабый	slack/weak	
слить	to bleed	
сломан	jammed	
сменить	to change	
стучит	knocking	
сухой	dry	
течет	leaking	
треснул	cracked	
уравновесить	to balance	
утечка	blowing	

Phase 4—Getting it fixed

Have you found the trouble?	**Вы нашли поломку?**	vi nah**shlyee** pah**lom**koo

Now that you know what's wrong, or at least have some idea, you'll want to find out …

Is that serious?	**Серьёзная поломка?**	syehr'**yoz**nahyah pah-**lom**kah
Can you fix it?	**Вы сможете исправить?**	vi s**mo**zhihtyee ees**prah**vyeet'
Can you do it now?	**Сможете исправить сразу?**	s**mo**zhityee ees**prah**vyeet' **srah**zoo
What's it going to cost?	**Сколько это будет стоить?**	**skol**'kah **eh**tah **boo**dyeet **sto**eet'
Have you the necessary spare parts?	**Запчасти у вас есть?**	zahp**chyahs**tyee oo vahss yehst'

What if he says "no"?

Why can't you do it?	Почему вы не можете исправить?	pahchyeemoo vi nyee mozhityee eesprahvyeet'
Is it essential to have that part?	Эта часть необходима?	ehtah chyast' nyeeahbkhadyeemah
How long is it going to take to get the spare parts?	Сколько нужно времени, чтобы достать запчасти?	skol'kah noozhnah vryehmyeenyee shtobi dahstaht' zahpchyahstyee
Where's the nearest garage that can repair it?	Где ближайшая станция обслуживания, где это могут исправить?	gdyeh blyeezhighshahyah stahntsiyah ahbsloozhivahn'yah gdyeh ehtah mogoot eesprahvyeet'
Well, can you fix it so that I can get as far as …?	Вы можете поправить так, чтобы мне доехать до…?	vi mozhityee pahprahvyeet' tahk shtobi mnyeh dahyehkhaht' dah

If you're really stuck, ask if you can leave the car at the garage. Contact the nearest Intourist representative. He'll help you out of the jam and will get you another car.

Settling the bill

Is everything fixed?	Всё готово?	vsyo gahtovah
How much do I owe you?	Сколько я вам должен?	skol'kah yah vahm dolzhin

The garage then presents you with a bill. If you're satisfied …

Do I pay you in rubles or Intourist coupons?	Платить рублями или талонами Интуриста?	plahtyeet' rooblyahmee eelyee tahlonahmee eentooreestah
Will you take a traveller's cheque (check)?	Берёте ли вы дорожные чеки?	byeeryotyee lyee vi dahrozhniyeh chyehkee
Thanks very much for your help.	Большое спасибо!	bahl'shoyeh spahsseebah
This is for you.	Это вам.	ehtah vahm

But you may feel that the workmanship is sloppy or that you're paying for work not done. Get the bill itemized. If necessary, get it translated before you pay.

| I would like to check the bill first. Will you itemize the work done? | Я хотел бы сперва посмотреть квитанцию. Пожалуйста, перечислите, что вы сделали. | yah khah**tyehl** bi spyehr**vah** pahsmaht**ryeht'** kveetahn-tsiyoo. pahz**hah**loostah pyeeryee**chees**lyeetyee shto vi **zdyeh**lahlyee |

If the garage still won't back down—and you're sure you're right—get the help of a third party.

Some international road signs

No vehicles

No entry

No overtaking
(passing)

Oncoming traffic
has priority

Maximum
speed limit

No parking

Caution

Intersection

Dangerous bend
(curve)

Road narrows

Intersection
with secondary
road

Two-way traffic

Dangerous hill

Uneven road

Falling rocks

Give way (yield)

Main road,
thoroughfare

End of restriction

One-way traffic

Traffic goes
this way

Roundabout
(rotary)

Bicycles only

Pedestrians
only

Minimum speed
limit

Keep right
(left if symbol
reversed)

Parking

Hospital

Motorway
(expressway)

Motor vehicles
only

Filling station

No through road

Doctor

Frankly, how much use is a phrase book going to be to you in case of serious injury or illness? The only phrase you need in such an emergency is:

Get a doctor – quick!	**Позовите врача – скорее!**	pahzah**vee**tyee vrah**chyah** – skah**ryeh**yeh

But there are minor aches and pains, ailments and irritations that can upset the best-planned trip. Here we can help you—and, perhaps, the doctor.

A few Soviet doctors will speak English well; others will know enough for your needs. But suppose there's something the doctor can't explain because of language difficulties? We've thought of that. As you'll see, this section has been arranged to enable you and the doctor to communicate. From page 165 to 171, you'll find your side of the dialogue on the upper half of each page; the doctor's is on the lower half.

The whole section has been divided into three parts: illness, wounds, nervous tension. Page 171 is concerned with prescriptions.

Medical treatment is free of charge in the Soviet Union, if the illness was contracted there. If taken ill in Moscow, you can go to the special clinic for foreigners at 3, Gruzinsky Lane, Block 2.

General

I need a doctor – quickly.	**Мне нужен врач – скорее!**	mnyeh **noo**zhin vrahch' – skah**ryeh**yeh
Is there a doctor in the hotel/house?	**Есть ли врач в гостинице/в доме?**	yehst' lyee vrahch' v gah-**styee**nyeetseh/v **do**myeh
Where's there a doctor who speaks English?	**Где найти врача, который говорит по-английски?**	gdyeh nigh**tyee** vrah**chyah** kah**to**riy gahvah**reet** pah ahng**lyeey**skee

Where's the surgery (doctor's office)/clinic?	Где кабинет врача/поликлиника?	gdyeh kahbee**nyeht** vrah**chyah**/pahlyeeklee-nyeekah
What are the doctor's consulting hours?	Когда приём?	kahg**dah** preey**om**
Could the doctor come and see me here?	Может ли врач прийти ко мне?	**mo**zheht lyee vrahch' preey-**tyee** kah mnyeh
What time can the doctor come?	В котором часу придёт врач?	v kah**to**rahm chyee**ssoo** pree**dyot** vrahch'

Symptoms

Use this section to tell the doctor what's wrong. Basically, what he'll require to know is:

What? (ache, pain, bruise, etc.)
Where? (arm, stomach, etc.)
How long? (have you had the trouble)

Before you visit the doctor, find out the answers to these questions by glancing through the pages that follow. In this way, you'll save time.

Parts of the body

ankle	лодыжка	lah**dizh**kah
appendix	апендикс	ah**pyehn**dyeeks
arm	рука	roo**kah**
artery	артерия	ahr**tyeh**reeyah
back	спина	spee**nah**
bladder	мочевой пузырь	mahch'eevoy poo**zir**'
blood	кровь	krov'
bone	кость	kost'
bowels	кишки	keesh**kee**
breast	грудь	grood'
cheek	щека	shchyeh**kah**
chest	грудная клетка	grood**nah**yah **klyeht**kah
chin	подбородок	pahdbah**ro**dahk
collar-bone	ключица	**klyoo**chyeetsah
ear	ухо	**oo**khah
elbow	локоть	**lo**kaht'
eye	глаз	glahz

DOCTOR

face	лицо	lyee**tso**
finger	палец	**pah**lyehts
foot	нога	nah**gah**
forehead	лоб	lob
gland	железа	zhilyee**zah**
hair	волосы	vo**lah**ssi
hand	рука	roo**kah**
head	голова	gahlah**vah**
heart	сердце	**syeh**rtseh
heel	пятка	**pyaht**kah
hip	бедро	byee**dro**
intestines	кишечник	kee**shehch**'nyeek
jaw	челюсть	**chyeh**lyoost'
joint	сустав	soo**stahv**
kidney	почка	**poch**'kah
knee	колено	kah**lyeh**nah
knee cap	коленная чашечка	kah**lyehn**nahyah **chyah**-shehch'kah
leg	нога	nah**gah**
lip	губа	goo**bah**
liver	печень	**pyeh**chyehn'
lung	лёгкие	**lyokh**keeyeh
mouth	рот	rot
muscle	мышца	**mish**tsah
neck	шея	**sheh**yah
nerve	нерв	nyehrv
nervous system	нервная система	**nyeh**rvnahyah sees**tyeh**-mah
nose	нос	noss
rib	ребро	ryee**bro**
shoulder	плечо	plyee**chyo**
skin	кожа	**ko**zhah
spine	позвоночник	pahzvah**noch**'nyeek
stomach	желудок	zhi**loo**dahk
tendon	сухожилие	sookhah**zhil**'yeh
thigh	бедро	byee**dro**
throat	горло	**gor**lah
thumb	большой палец	bahl'**shoy pah**lyehts
toe	палец на ноге	**pah**lyehts nah nah**ghyeh**
tongue	язык	yah**zik**
tonsils	миндалины	meen**dah**lyeeni
urine	моча	mah**chyah**
vein	вена	**vyeh**nah
wrist	запястье	zah**pyahst**'yeh

PATIENT

Part 1—Illness

I'm not feeling well.	Я плохо себя чувствую.	yah plokhah syeebyah chyoostvooyoo
I'm ill.	Я болен.	yah bolyehn
I've got a pain here.	Тут болит.	toot bahlyeet
His/Her ... hurts.	У него/У неё болит...	oo nyeevo/oo nyeeyo bahlyeet
I've got a ...	У меня...	oo myeenyah
headache	головная боль	gahlahvnahyah bol'
backache	боль в спине	bol' v speenyeh
fever	температура	tyeempyeerahtoorah
sore throat	болит горло	bahlyeet gorlah
I'm constipated.	У меня запор.	oo myeenyah zahpor
I've been vomiting.	Меня рвёт.	myeenyah rvyot

DOCTOR

DOCTOR

Болезнь

Что случилось?	What's the trouble?
Что у вас болит?	Where does it hurt?
Давно болит?	How long have you had this pain?
Давно вы это ощущаете?	How long have you been feeling like this?
Засучите рукав.	Roll up your sleeve.
Разденьтесь, пожалуйста (до пояса).	Please undress (down to the waist).
Снимите, пожалуйста, брюки и нижнее бельё.	Please remove your trousers and underpants.

PATIENT

I feel ill.	**Я болен.**	yah **bol**yehn
I feel faint.	**У меня дурнота.**	oo myee**nyah** doornah**tah**
I feel nauseated.	**Меня тошнит.**	myee**nyah** tahsh**nyeet**
I feel shivery.	**У меня озноб.**	oo myee**nyah** ahz**nob**
I/He's/She's got (a/an) …	**У меня/У него/ У неё…**	oo myee**nyah**/oo nyee**evo** oo nyee**yo**
abscess	**нарыв**	nah**riv**
asthma	**одышка**	ah**dish**kah
boil	**фурункул**	foo**roon**kool
chill	**простуда**	prah**stoo**dah
cold	**простуда**	prah**stoo**dah
constipation	**запор**	zah**por**
convulsions	**судороги**	**soo**dahrahghee
cramps	**спазмы**	**spahz**mi
diarrhea	**понос**	pah**noss**
fever	**температура**	tyeempyeerah**too**rah
haemorrhoids	**геморрой**	ghyeemah**roy**
hay fever	**сенная лихорадка**	syeen**nah**yah lyeekhah-**rahd**kah

DOCTOR

Ложитесь сюда, пожалуйста.	Please lie down over here.
Откройте рот.	Open your mouth.
Сделайте глубокий вдох.	Breathe deeply.
Кашляните, пожалуйста.	Cough, please.
Я вам измерю температуру.	I'll take your temperature.
Я вам измерю давление.	I'm going to take your blood pressure.
Это у вас впервые?	Is this the first time you've had this?
Я вам сделаю укол.	I'll give you an injection.
Я возьму у вас мочу на анализ.	I want a specimen of your urine.

PATIENT

hernia	грыжа	**gri**zhah
indigestion	расстройство желудка	rahs**stroy**stvah zhi**lood**kah
inflammation of ...	воспаление...	vahspah**lyehn**'yeh
influenza	грипп	greep
morning sickness	тошнота по утрам	tahsh**nah**tah pah oo**trahm**
stiff neck	надуло шею	nah**doo**lah **sheh**yoo
rheumatism	ревматизм	ryehvmah**tyeezm**
sunburn	солнечный ожог	**sol**nyeech'niy ah**zhog**
sunstroke	солнечный удар	**sol**nyeech'niy oo**dahr**
tonsillitis	воспаление миндалин	vahspah**lyehn**'yeh meen-**dah**lyeen
ulcer	язва	**yahz**van
whooping cough	коклюш	kahk**lyoosh**
It's nothing serious, I hope?	Ничего серьёзного, правда?	nyee**chyeevo** syeer'**yoz**-nahvah **prahv**dah
I'd like you to prescribe me some medicine.	Пропишите мне, пожалуйста, лекарство.	prahpee**shit**yee mnyeh pah**zhah**loostah lyee-**kahr**stvah

---

DOCTOR

Ничего серьёзного.	It's nothing to worry about.
Вы должны ... дней полежать в постели.	You must stay in bed for ... days.
У вас...	You've got ...
простуда/артрит/воспаление лёгких/грипп/отравление/воспаление...	a cold/arthritis/pneumonia/influenza/food poisoning/an inflammation of ...
Вы слишком много курите/пьёте.	You're smoking/drinking too much.
Вы переутомились. Вам нужен покой.	You're over-tired. You need a rest.
Я вас пошлю к специалисту.	I want you to see a specialist.
Я вас направлю в стационар на исследования.	I want you to go to the hospital for a general check-up.
Я вам назначу антибиотики.	I'll prescribe an antibiotic.

PATIENT

I'm a diabetic.	У меня диабет.	oo myee**nyah** dyeeah**byeht**
I've a cardiac condition.	У меня больное сердце.	oo myee**nyah** bahl'**noyeh syeh**rtseh
I had a heart attack in …	У меня был сердечный приступ в …	oo myee**nyah** bil syeer-**dyehch**'niy **pree**stoop v
I'm allergic to …	Я не переношу…	yah nyee pyeereenah**shoo**
This is my usual medicine.	Я обычно принимаю это лекарство.	yah ah**bich**'nah preenyee-**mahyoo eh**tah lyee**kahrst**vah
I need this medicine.	Мне нужно это лекарство.	mnyeh **noozh**nah **eh**tah lyee**kahr**stvah
I'm expecting a baby.	Я беременна.	yah byee**ryeh**myeenah
Can I travel?	Можно ли мне продолжать путешествие?	**mozh**nah lyee mnyeh prahdahl**zhaht'** pootyee-**shehst**vyeeyeh

---

DOCTOR

Сколько вы принимаете инсулина?	What dose of insulin are you taking?
Уколы или стоматически?	Injection or oral?
Какое вы принимали лекарство?	What medicine have you been taking?
У вас (лёгкий) сердечный приступ.	You've had a (slight) heart attack.
У нас в Советском Союзе… нет. Это почти такое же лекарство.	We don't use … in the Soviet Union. This is very similar.
Когда вы ждёте ребёнка?	When is the baby due?
Вы можете продолжать путешествие до…	You can't travel until….

PATIENT

Part 2—Wounds

Could you have a look at this ...?	Посмотрите, пожалуйста, этот...	pahsmahtreetyee pahzhahloostah ehtaht
blister	волдырь	vahldir'
boil	фурункул	fooroonkool
bruise	ушиб	ooshib
burn	ожог	ahzhog
cut	порез	pahryehz
graze	ссадину	s-sahdyeenoo
insect bite	укус насекомого	ookooss nahssyeekomahvah
lump	шишку	shishkoo
rash	сыпь	sip'
sting	укус	ookooss
swelling	опухоль	opookhahl'
wound	рану	rahnoo
I can't move my .. It hurts.	Я не могу двигать... она/он болит.	yah nyee mahgoo dvyeegaht' ... ahnah/on bahlyeet

DOCTOR

Раны

Есть заражение (заражения нет).	It's (not) infected.
Я хочу сделать вам рентген.	I want you to have an X-ray.
Он/она...	It's ...
сломан/растянут вывихнут/разорван	broken/sprained dislocated/torn
Вы растянули мышцу.	You've pulled a muscle.
Я вам дам антисептическое средство. Ничего опасного нет.	I'll give you an antiseptic. It's not serious.
Придите ко мне через... дней.	I want you to come and see me in ... days' time.

PATIENT

Part 3—Nervous tension

I'm in a nervous state.	У меня не в порядке нервы.	oo myee**nyah** nyee v pahr**yahd**keh **nyeh**rvi
I'm feeling depressed.	У меня депрессия.	oo myee**nyah** deh**prehss**yeeyah
I want some sleeping pills.	Мне нужно снотворное.	mnyeh **noozh**nah snah**tvor**nahyeh
I can't eat/sleep.	Я не ем/не сплю.	yah nyee yehm/nyee splyoo
I'm having nightmares.	У меня кошмары.	oo myee**nyah** kahsh**mah**ri
Can you prescribe a …?	Пропишите мне, пожалуйста …	prahpyee**shi**tyee mnyeh pah**zhah**loostah
sedative anti-depressant	успокоительное средство против депрессии	oospahkah**hee**tyeel'nahyeh **sryehd**stvah prot**yeev** deh**prehss**syeeyee

DOCTOR

Нервное расстройство

У вас нервное расстройство.	You're suffering from nervous tension.
Вам нужен покой.	You need a rest.
Какие таблетки вы принимаете?	What tablets have you been taking?
Сколько таблеток в день?	How many a day?
Давно вы себя так чувствуете?	How long have you been feeling like this?
Я вам пропишу таблетки	I'll prescribe some pills.
Я вам дам успокоительное.	I'll give you a sedative.

PATIENT

Prescription and dosage

What kind of medicine is this?	Какое это лекарство?	kahkoyeh ehtah lyeekahrstvah
How many times a day should I take it?	Сколько раз в день принимать?	skol'kah rahz v dyehn' preenyeemaht'
Must I swallow them whole?	По целой таблетке?	pah tsehligh tahblyehtkeh
Do all chemists' (drugstores) carry this medicine in stock?	Это лекарство можно купить в любой аптеке?	ehtah lyeekahrstvah mozhnah koopeet' v lyooboy ahptyehkyeh
Where is the best chemist's in town?	Где самая лучшая аптека города?	gdyeh sahmahyah loochshahyah ahptyehkah gorahdah
Is this prescription expensive?	Это лекарство дорогое?	ehtah lyeekahrstvah dahrahgoyeh
Thanks for your help, Doctor.	Спасибо за помощь, доктор.	spahsseebah zah pomahshch' doktahr

DOCTOR

Лекарства и дозы

Принимайте это лекарство по... чайных ложки каждые... часа.	Take ... teaspoonful of this medicine every ... hours.
Принимайте по ... таблетки, запивайте водой...	Take ...tablets with a glass of water ...
... раз в день	... times a day
перед каждой едой	before each meal
после каждой еды	after each meal
утром	in the mornings
вечером	at night

Dentist

Can you recommend a good dental clinic?	Не знаете ли вы хорошую стоматологическую поликлинику?	nyee **znah**eetyee lyee vi khah**roh**shooyoo stah-mahtah**lahghee**chyehskoo-yoo pahlyee**klyee**enyeekoo
What are the hours there?	Когда там приём?	kah**gdah** tahm pree**yom**
How long will I have to wait?	Сколько мне придётся ждать?	**skol**'kah mnyeh pree**dyo**tsah zhdaht'
I think it's my turn to see the dentist.	Теперь моя очередь.	tyee**pyehr**' mah**yah ochyee**ryehd'
I have a toothache.	У меня болит зуб.	oo myee**nyah** bah**lyeet** zoob
I have an abscess.	У меня нарыв.	oo myee**nyah nah**riv
This tooth hurts.	Этот зуб болит.	**eh**taht zoob bah**lyeet**
at the top at the bottom in the front at the back	сверху снизу впереди сзади	**svyeh**rkhoo **snyee**zoo vpyeeryee**dyee** **szah**dyee
Can you fix it temporarily?	Нельзя ли залечить это временно?	nyeel'**zyah** lyee zah**lyee**chyeet' **eh**taht **vryeh**myeennah
I don't want it extracted (pulled).	Если возможно, зуб не вырывайте.	**yehs**lyee vah**zmozh**nah zoob nyee viri**vigh**tyee
I have lost a filling.	Выпала пломба.	vi**pah**lah **plom**bah
The gum is very sore/ The gum is bleeding.	Десна очень воспалена/Десна кровоточит.	dyees**nah och**yeen' vahs-pah**lyee**nah/dyees**nah** krahvah**tah**chyeet

Dentures

I have broken this denture.	Я сломал протез.	yah slah**mahl** prah**tehz**
Can you repair this denture?	Можно починить этот протез?	**mozh**nah pahchyee**nyeet**' **eh**taht prah**tehz**
When will it be ready?	Когда он будет готов?	kah**gdah** on **boo**dyeet gah**tov**

Optician

I've broken my glasses.	Я сломал очки.	yah slah**mahl** ahch'**kee**
Can you repair them for me?	Можно их починить?	**mozh**nah eekh pahchyee**nyeet'**
When will they be ready?	Когда они будут готовы?	kahg**dah** ahn**yee boo**doot gah**tovi**
Can you change the lenses?	Можно ли переменить стёкла?	**mozh**nah lyee pyeeryee-myee**nyeet' styok**lah
I want some sun-glasses.	Мне нужны тёмные очки.	mnyeh nooz**hni tyom**niyeh ahch'**kee**
I'd like to buy a pair of binoculars.	Я хотел бы купить бинокль.	yah khah**tyehl** bi koo**peet' bee**nokl'
How much do I owe you?	Сколько я вам должен?	**skol'**kah yah vahm **dol**zhin

Reference section

Where do you come from?

This page will help you to explain where you're from, where you've been and where you're going.

Africa	Африка	ahfreekah
Australia	Австралия	ahvstrahlyeeyah
Austria	Австрия	ahvstreeyah
Belgium	Бельгия	byehl'gheeyah
Bulgaria	Болгария	bahlgahreeyah
Canada	Канада	kahnahdah
China	Китай	keetigh
Czechoslovakia	Чехословакия	chyehkhahslahvahkeeyah
England	Англия	ahnglyeeyah
Europe	Европа	yehvropah
Finland	Финляндия	feenlyahndyeeyah
France	Франция	frahntsiyah
Germany	Германия	ghyehrmahnyeeyah
Great Britain	Великобритания	vyehlyeekahbryeetah- nyeeyah
Hungary	Венгрия	vyehngreeyah
Ireland	Ирландия	eerlahndyeeyah
Japan	Япония	yahponyeeyah
Netherlands	Голландия	gahlahndyeeyah
New Zealand	Новая Зеландия	novahyah zyeelahndyeeyah
Norway	Норвегия	nahrvyehgheeyah
Poland	Польша	pol'shah
Romania	Румыния	roominyeeyah
Scandinavia	Скандинавия	skahndyeenahveeyah
Scotland	Шотландия	shahtlahndyeeyah
South Africa	Южная Африка	yoozhnahyah ahfreekah
Sweden	Швеция	shvyehtsiyah
Switzerland	Швейцария	shvyaytsahreeyah
Turkey	Турция	toortsiyah
USA	Соединённые Штаты Америки	sahyeedyeenyonniyeh shtahti ahmyehreekee
USSR	Союз Советских Социалистических Республик	sahyooz sahvyehtskeekh sahtsiahlyeestyeechyees- keekh ryeespooblyeek
Yugoslavia	Югославия	yoogahslahveeyah
Wales	Уэльс	ooehl's

Numbers

1	один	ah**dyeen**
2	два	dvah
3	три	tree
4	четыре	chyee**ti**ryeh
5	пять	pyaht'
6	шесть	shehst'
7	семь	syehm'
8	восемь	**vo**ssyeem'
9	девять	**dyeh**vyaht'
10	десять	**dyeh**ssyaht'
11	одиннадцать	ah**dyeen**nahtsaht'
12	двенадцать	dvee**naht**saht'
13	тринадцать	tree**naht**saht'
14	четырнадцать	chyee**tir**nahtsaht'
15	пятнадцать	pyee**naht**saht'
16	шестнадцать	shis**naht**saht'
17	семнадцать	syeem**naht**saht'
18	восемнадцать	vahssyeem**naht**saht'
19	девятнадцать	dyeevyeet**naht**saht'
20	двадцать	**dvah**tsaht'
21	двадцать один	**dvah**tsaht' ah**dyeen**
22	двадцать два	**dvah**tsaht' dvah
23	двадцать три	**dvah**tsaht' tree
24	двадцать четыре	**dvah**tsaht' chyee**ti**ryeh
25	двадцать пять	**dvah**tsaht' pyaht'
26	двадцать шесть	**dvah**tsaht' shehst'
27	двадцать семь	**dvah**tsaht' syehm'
28	двадцать восемь	**dvah**tsaht' **vo**ssyeem'
29	двадцать девять	**dvah**tsaht' **dyeh**vyaht'
30	тридцать	**tree**tsaht'
31	тридцать один	**tree**tsaht' ah**dyeen**
32	тридцать два	**tree**tsaht' dvah
33	тридцать три	**tree**tsaht' tree
40	сорок	**so**rahk
41	сорок один	**so**rahk ah**dyeen**
42	сорок два	**so**rahk dvah
43	сорок три	**so**rahk tree
50	пятьдесят	peedyee**ssyaht**
51	пятьдесят один	peedyee**ssyaht** ah**dyeen**
52	пятьдесят два	peedyee**ssyaht** dvah
53	пятьдесят три	peedyee**ssyaht** tree
60	шестьдесят	shisdyee**ssyaht**
61	шестьдесят один	shisdyee**ssyaht** ah**dyeen**
62	шестьдесят два	shisdyee**ssyaht** dvah

63	шестьдесят три	shisdyee**ssyaht** tree
70	семьдесят	**syehm**dyeessyaht
71	семьдесят один	**syehm**dyeessyaht ah**dyeen**
72	семьдесят два	**syehm**dyeessyaht dvah
73	семьдесят три	**syehm**dyeessyaht tree
80	восемьдесят	vossyeemdyeessyaht
81	восемьдесят один	**vo**ssyeemdyeessyaht ah**dyeen**
82	восемьдесят два	**vo**ssyeemdyeessyaht dvah
83	восемьдесят три	**vo**ssyeemdyeessyaht tree
90	девяносто	dyeevyeenostah
91	девяносто один	dyeevyeenostah ah**dyeen**
92	девяносто два	dyeevyeenostah dvah
93	девяносто три	dyeevyeenostah tree
100	сто	sto
101	сто один	sto ah**dyeen**
102	сто два	sto dvah
110	сто десять	sto **dyeh**ssyaht'
120	сто двадцать	sto **dvah**tsaht'
130	сто тридцать	sto **tree**tsaht'
140	сто сорок	sto **so**rahk
150	сто пятьдесят	sto pyeedyee**ssyaht**
160	сто шестьдесят	sto shisdyee**ssyaht**
170	сто семьдесят	sto **syehm**dyeessyaht
180	сто восемьдесят	sto **vo**ssyeemdyeessyaht
190	сто девяносто	sto dyeevyeenostah
200	двести	**dvyeh**stye
300	триста	**tree**stah
400	четыреста	chyee**tir**yeestah
500	пятьсот	pyeet**sot**
600	шестьсот	shis**sot**
700	семьсот	syeem**sot**
800	восемьсот	**vo**ssyeem**sot**
900	девятьсот	dyeevyeet**sot**
1000	тысяча	**ti**ssyeechyah
1100	тысяча сто	**ti**ssyeechyah sto
1200	тысяча двести	**ti**ssyeechyah **dvyeh**stye
2000	две тысячи	dvyeh **ti**ssyeechye
5000	пять тысяч	pyaht' **ti**ssyeech'
10,000	десять тысяч	**dyeh**ssyaht' **ti**ssyeech'
50,000	пятьдесят тысяч	peedyee**ssyaht ti**ssyeech'
100,000	сто тысяч	sto **ti**ssyeech'
1,000,000	миллион	meely**ee**on
1,000,000,000	миллиард	meelyee**ahrd**

first	первый	**pyehr**viy
second	второй	vtah**roy**
third	третий	**tryeht**yeey
fourth	четвёртый	chyeet**vy**ortiy
fifth	пятый	**pyah**tiy
sixth	шестой	shis**toy**
seventh	седьмой	syeed'**moy**
eighth	восьмой	vahs'**moy**
ninth	девятый	dyee**vyah**tiy
tenth	десятый	dyee**ssyah**tiy
once	один раз	ah**dyeen** rahz
twice	дважды	**dvahzh**di
three times	трижды	**treezh**di
a half	половина	pahlah**vee**nah
half a ...	половина...	pahlah**vee**nah
half of ...	половина...	pahlah**vee**nah
half (adj.)	пол	pol
a quarter	четверть	**chyeht**vyehrt'
one third	треть	**tryeht'**
a pair of	пара	**pah**rah
a dozen	дюжина	**dyoo**zhinah
1985	тысяча девятьсот восемьдесят пять	**tis**syeechyah dyeevyee**tsot vos**syeemdyee**ssyaht** pyaht'
1987	тысяча девятьсот восемьдесят семь	**tis**syeechyah dyeevyee**tsot vos**syeemdyee**ssyaht** syehm'
1990	тысяча девятьсот девяносто	**tis**syeechyah dyeevyee**tsot** dyeevyee**nos**tah

Time

четверть первого

(**chyeht**vyehrt' **pyehr**vahvah)

двадцать минут второго

(**dvah**tsaht' mee**noot** vtah**ro**vah)

двадцать пять минут третьего

(**dvah**tsaht' pyaht' mee-**noot** tryeht'yeevah)

половина четвёртого

(pahlah**vee**nah chyeet**vyor**tahvah)

без двадцати пяти пять

(byehz dvahtsah**tyee** pyee**tyee** pyaht')

без двадцати шесть

(byehz dvahtsah**tyee** shehst')

без четверти семь

(byehz **chyeht**-vyehrtyee syehm')

без десяти восемь

(byehz dyeessyee-**tyee vo**ssyeem')

без пяти девять

(byehz pyee**tyee dyeh**vyaht')

десять часов

(**dyeh**ssyah' chyee**ssov**)

пять минут двенадцатого

(pyaht' mee**noot** dvee**nah**tsahtahvah)

десять минут первого

(**dyeh**ssyah' mee**noot pyehr**vahvah)

REFERENCE SECTION

Have you got the time?

What time is it?	**Который час?**	kah**to**riy chyahss
It's…	**Сейчас…**	see**chyahss**
Excuse me. Can you tell me the time?	**Вы не скажете, который час?**	vi nyee s**kah**zhityee kah**to**riy chyahss
I'll meet you at … tomorrow.	**Встретимся завтра в…**	v**stryeh**tyeemsah **zahv**trah v
I'm sorry I'm late.	**Простите за опоздание.**	prah**styee**tyee zah ahpahz**dahn**'yeh
At what time does … open?	**Когда открывается…?**	kahg**dah** ahtkri**vah**eetsah
At what time does … close?	**Когда закрывается…?**	kahg**dah** zakri**vah**eetsah
How long will it last?	**Сколько это займёт?**	skol'kah **eh**tah zigh**myot**
What time will it end?	**Когда это кончится?**	kahg**dah** **eh**tah **kon**chyeetsah
At what time should I be there?	**Когда я должен там быть?**	kahg**dah** yah **dol**zhin tahm bit'
At what time will you be there?	**Когда вы там будете?**	kahg**dah** vi tahm **boo**dyeetyee
Can I come …?	**Можно мне прийти…**	**mozh**nah mnyeh preey**tyee**
at 8 o'clock	**в восемь часов**	v **vos**seyem' chyees**sov**
at 2:30	**в половине третьего**	v pahlah**vyee**nyee **tryeh**t'yeevah
after/afterwards	**после/потом**	pos**lyee**/pah**tom**
before/beforehand	**до/раньше**	do/**rahn**'shi
early	**рано**	**rah**nah
in time	**во-время**	**vo**vreemyah
late	**поздно**	**poz**nah
midnight	**полночь**	**pol**nahch'
noon	**полдень**	**pol**dyehn
hour	**час**	chyahss
minute	**минута**	mee**noo**tah
second	**секунда**	see**koon**dah
quarter of an hour	**четверть часа**	**chyeh**tvyehrt' chyees**sah**
half an hour	**полчаса**	polchyees**sah**

REFERENCE SECTION

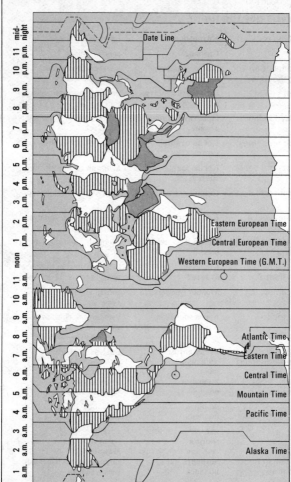

Countries which have adopted a time differing from that in the corresponding time zone. Also note that in the USSR, official time is one hour ahead of the time in each corresponding time zone. In summer, numerous countries advance time one hour ahead of standard time.

Date Line

Eastern European Time

Central European Time

Western European Time (G.M.T.)

Atlantic Time

Eastern Time

Central Time

Mountain Time

Pacific Time

Alaska Time

Days

What day is it today?	Какой сегодня день?	kahkoy syeevodnyah dyehn'
Sunday	воскресенье	vahskryeessyehn'yeh
Monday	понедельник	pahnyeedyehl'nyeek
Tuesday	вторник	vtornyeek
Wednesday	среда	sryeedah
Thursday	четверг	chyeetvyehrg
Friday	пятница	pyahtnyeetsah
Saturday	суббота	soobotah

Note: In Russian, names of days and months don't require a capital letter.

in the morning	утром	ootrahm
during the day	днём	dnyom
in the afternoon	после обеда	poslyeh ahbyehdah
in the evening	вечером	vyehchyeerahm
at night	ночью	noch'yoo

yesterday	вчера	vchyeerah
today	сегодня	syeevodnyah
tomorrow	завтра	zahvtrah
the day before	за день до	zah dyehn' dah
the next day	на другой день	nah droogoy dyehn'
two days ago	два дня тому назад	dvah dnyah tahmoo nahzahd
in three days' time	через три дня	chyehryehz tree dnyah
last week	на прошлой неделе	nah proshligh nyeedyehlyee
next week	на следующей неделе	nah slyehdooshchyay nyeedyehlyee
for two weeks	на две недели	nah dvyeh nyeedyehlyee

birthday	день рождения	dyehn' rahzhdyehn'yah
day	день	dyehn'
day off	выходной день	vikhahdnoy dyehn'
holiday	праздник	prahznyeek
holidays (vacation)	отпуск	otpoosk
month	месяц	myehssyahts
school holidays	каникулы	kahnyeekooli
week	неделя	nyeedyehlyah
weekday	будний день	boodnyee dyehn'
weekend	конец недели	kahnyehts nyeedyehlyee
working day	рабочий день	rahbochyeey dyehn'

Months

January	январь	yeen**vahr'**
February	февраль	fyee**vrahl'**
March	март	mahrt
April	апрель	ahp**ryehl'**
May	май	migh
June	июнь	eeyoon'
July	июль	eeyool'
August	август	**ahv**goost
September	сентябрь	syeen'**tyahbr'**
October	октябрь	ahk**tyahbr'**
November	ноябрь	nah**yahbr'**
December	декабрь	dyee**kahbr'**

since June	с июня	s eeyoonyah
during the month of August	в августе	v **ahv**goostyeh
last month	прошлый месяц	**prosh**liy **myeh**ssyahts
next month	следующий месяц	**slyeh**dooshchyeey **myeh**ssyahts
the month before	месяц тому назад	**myeh**ssyahts tah**moo** nah**zahd**
the month after	через месяц	**chyeh**ryehz **myeh**ssyahts
July 1	первое июля	**pyehr**vahyeh eeyoolyah
March 17	семнадцатое марта	syeem**naht**sahtahyeh **mahr**tah

Letter headings are written thus:

Moscow, August 17, 19..	Москва, 17 августа 19..
Kiev, July 1, 19..	Киев, 1 июля 19..

Seasons

spring	весна	**vyees**nah
summer	лето	**lyeh**tah
autumn	осень	**ossyeen'**
winter	зима	**zee**mah

in spring	весной	vyees**noy**
during the summer	летом	**lyeh**tahm
in autumn	осенью	**ossyeen'yoo**
during the winter	зимой	zee**moy**

REFERENCE SECTION

Public holidays

These are the main public holidays in the Soviet Union when banks, offices and shops are closed:

January 1   New Year's Day
March 8   Women's Day
May 1, 2   Labour Days
May 9   Victory Day
October 7   Constitution Day
November 7 and 8   October Revolution Days

The year round...

Here are the average temperatures for some Soviet cities (in degrees Fahrenheit):

	Moscow	Leningrad	Kiev	Astrakhan
January	14	18	21	19
February	17	18	23	23
March	25	25	31	33
April	39	37	44	48
May	55	49	58	64
June	61	58	63	73
July	66	63	67	77
August	62	60	65	74
September	51	51	56	63
October	40	41	45	49
November	28	30	33	36
December	19	22	26	27

Common abbreviations

Here are some Russian abbreviations you are likely to encounter.

в.	вольт	volt
г.	год	year
г.	город	city
г.	грамм	gramme
др.	доктор	doctor
д.	дом	house
ж.	женский	women
и.т.д.	и так далее	etc.
км.	километр	kilometre
коп.	копейка	kopeck
л.	литр	litre
м.	метр	metre
м.	мужской	men
наб.	набережная	quay, pier
п/х.	пароход	steamship
пер.	переулок	lane
пл.	площадь	square
пр.	проспект	avenue
проф.	профессор	professor
р.	рубль	ruble
сек.	секунда	second
см.	смотри	see
с.	сорт	sort, grade
СССР		USSR
тов.	товарищ	comrade
ул.	улица	street
ч.	час	hour
шт.	штука	piece, item

Conversion tables

Centimetres and inches

To change centimetres into inches, multiply by .39.

To change inches into centimetres, multiply by 2.54.

	in.	feet	yards
1 mm	0,039	0,003	0,001
1 cm	0,39	0,03	0,01
1 dm	3,94	0,32	0,10
1 m	39,40	3,28	1,09

	mm	cm	m
1 in.	25,4	2,54	0,025
1 ft.	304,8	30,48	0,304
1 yd.	914,4	91,44	0,914

(32 metres = 35 yards)

Temperature

To convert Centigrade into degrees Fahrenheit, multiply Centigrade by 1.8 and add 32.

To convert degrees Fahrenheit into Centigrade, subtract 32 from Fahrenheit and divide by 1.8.

Metres and feet

The figure in the middle stands for both metres and feet, e.g.,
1 metre = 3.281 ft. and 1 foot = 0.30 m.

Metres		Feet
0.30	1	3.281
0.61	2	6.563
0.91	3	9.843
1.22	4	13.124
1.52	5	16.403
1.83	6	19.686
2.13	7	22.967
2.44	8	26.248
2.74	9	29.529
3.05	10	32.810
3.35	11	36.091
3.66	12	39.372
3.96	13	42.635
4.27	14	45.934
4.57	15	49.215
4.88	16	52.496
5.18	17	55.777
5.49	18	59.058
5.79	19	62.339
6.10	20	65.620
7.62	25	82.023
15.24	50	164.046
22.86	75	246.069
30.48	100	328.092

Other conversion charts

REFERENCE SECTION

Weight conversion

The figure in the middle stands for both kilograms and pounds, e.g., 1 kilogram = 2.205 lb. and 1 pound = 0.45 kilograms.

Kilograms (kg.)		Avoirdupois pounds
0.45	1	2.205
0.90	2	4.405
1.35	3	6.614
1.80	4	8.818
2.25	5	11.023
2.70	6	13.227
3.15	7	15.432
3.60	8	17.636
4.05	9	19.840
4.50	10	22.045
6.75	15	33.068
9.00	20	44.889
11.25	25	55.113
22.50	50	110.225
33.75	75	165.338
45.00	100	220.450

REFERENCE SECTION

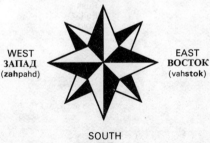

NORTH
СЕВЕР
(syehvyehr)

WEST
ЗАПАД
(zahpahd)

EAST
ВОСТОК
(vahstok)

SOUTH
ЮГ
(yoog)

What does that sign mean?

You're sure to encounter some of these signs and notices on your trip:

Без стука не входить	Knock before entering
Берегись	Caution
Вход	Entrance
Входа нет	No entrance
Вход свободный	Free entrance
Выход	Exit
Горячая	Hot
Женский	Ladies
Закрыто	Closed
За нарушение штраф	Trespassers will be prosecuted
Занято	Reserved, occupied
Запасной выход	Emergency exit
…запрещается	… forbidden
Звоните	Please ring
Касса	Cashier
Лифт	Lift (elevator)
Мужской	Gentlemen
Не курить	No smoking
Опасно для жизни	Danger of death
Осторожно собака	Beware of the dog
Посторонним вход воспрещён	Private
Распродано	To let, for hire
Руками не трогать	Do not touch
Свободно	Vacant
Справочное бюро	Information
Толкайте	Push
Тяните	Pull
Холодная	Cold

Emergency

By the time the emergency is upon you it's too late to turn to this page to find the Russian for "I'll scream if you …". So have a look at this short list beforehand—and, if you want to be on the safe side, learn the expressions shown in capitals.

Be quick	Скорее	skahryehyeh
Call the police	Позовите милицию	pahzahveetyee meelyeetsiyoo
CAREFUL	ОСТОРОЖНО	ahstahrozhnah
Come here	Идите сюда	eedyeetyee syoodah
Come in	Входите	vkhahdyeetyee
Danger	Опасно	ahpahsnah
Fire	Пожар	pahzhahr
Gas	Газ	gahz
Get a doctor	Позовите врача	pahzahveetyee vrahchyah
Go away	Уходите	ookhahdyeetyee
HELP	НА ПОМОЩЬ	nah pomahshch'
Get help quickly	Позовите быстро кого-нибудь на помощь	pahzahveetyee bistrah kahvonyeebood' nah pomahshch'
I'm ill	Я болен	yah bolyehn
I'm lost	Я заблудился	yah zahbloodyeelsah
I've lost …	Я потерял …	yah pahtyeeryahl
Leave me alone	Оставьте меня	ahstahvtyee myeenyah
Lie down	Ложитесь	lahzhityees
Listen	Слушайте	slooshightyee
Listen to me	Послушайте меня	pahslooshightyee myeenyah
Look	Посмотрите	pahsmahtreetyee
LOOK OUT	ОСТОРОЖНО	ahstahrozhnah
POLICE	МИЛИЦИЯ	meelyeetsiyah
Quick	Быстро	bistrah
STOP	СТОЙ	stoy
Stop here	Стойте тут	stoytyee toot
Stop that man	Держи его	dyehrzhi yeevo
STOP THIEF	ДЕРЖИ ВОРА	dyehrzhi vorah
Stop or I'll scream	Перестаньте, а то я закричу	pyeereestahn'tyee ahto yah zahkreechyoo

FOR CAR ACCIDENTS, see page 149

REFERENCE SECTION

Index

Quick reference page

Please.	Пожалуйста.	pahzhahloostah
Thank you.	Спасибо.	spahsseebah
Yes/No.	Да/Нет.	dah/nyeht
Excuse me.	Простите/Извините.	prahstyeetyee/eezvee-nyeetyee
Waiter, please.	Официант!	ahfeetsiahnt
How much is that?	Сколько это будет?	skol'kah ehtah boodyeet
Where are the toilets?	Где туалет?	gdyeh tooahlyeht

туалет (tooahlyeht)	Toilets
М (moozhskoy) GENTLEMEN	**Ж** (zhehnskeey) LADIES

Could you tell me …?	Скажите, пожа-луйста …	skahzhityee pahzhah-loostah
where/when/why	где/когда/почему	gdyeh/kahgdah/pahchyee-moo
Help me, please.	Помогите мне, пожалуйста.	pahmahgheetyee mnyeh pahzhahloostah
What time is it?	Который час?	kahtoriy chyahss
one/first two/second three/third	один/первый два/второй три/третий	ahdyeen/pyehrviy dvah/vtahroy tree/tryehtyeey
What does this mean? I don't under-stand.	Что это значит? Я не понимаю.	shto ehtat znahchyeet yah nyee pahnyeemahyoo
Do you speak English?	Вы говорите по-английски?	vi gahvahreetyee pah ahnglyeeyskee

Say BERLITZ®

... and most people think of outstanding language schools.
But Berlitz has also become the world's leading publisher
of books for travellers – Travel Guides, Phrase Books,
Dictionaries – plus Cassettes and
Self-teaching courses.

Informative, accurate, up-to-date,
Books from Berlitz are written
with freshness and style. They
also slip easily into pocket or
purse – no need for bulky,
old-fashioned volumes.

Join the millions who know
how to travel. Whether for
fun or business, put Berlitz
in your pocket.

BERLITZ®

Leader in
Books and Cassettes
for Travellers

A Macmillan Company

BERLITZ® Books for travellers

TRAVEL GUIDES

They fit your pocket in both size and price. Modern, up-to-date, Berlitz gets all the information you need into 128 lively pages – 192 or 256 pages for country guides – with colour maps and photos throughout. What to see and do, where to shop, what to eat and drink, how to save.

AFRICA	Algeria (256 pages)* Kenya Morocco South Africa Tunisia
ASIA, MIDDLE EAST	China (256 pages) Hong Kong India (256 pages) Japan (256 pages) Nepal* Singapore Sri Lanka Thailand Egypt Jerusalem & Holy Land Saudi Arabia
AUSTRAL-ASIA	Australia (256 pages) New Zealand
BRITISH ISLES	Channel Islands London Ireland Oxford and Stratford Scotland
BELGIUM	Brussels
FRANCE	Brittany France (256 pages) French Riviera Loire Valley Normandy Paris
GERMANY	Berlin Munich The Rhine Valley
AUSTRIA and SWITZER-LAND	Tyrol Vienna Switzerland (192 pages)
GREECE, CYPRUS & TURKEY	Athens Corfu Crete Rhodes Greek Islands of Aegean Peloponnese Salonica/North. Greece Cyprus Istanbul/Aegean Coast Turkey (192 pages)
ITALY and MALTA	Florence Italian Adriatic Italian Riviera Italy (256 pages) Rome Sicily Venice Malta
NETHER-LANDS and SCANDI-NAVIA	Amsterdam Copenhagen Helsinki Oslo and Bergen Stockholm

*in preparation